OUTSIDE
the
SOUTHERN
MYTH

OUTSIDE

the

SOUTHERN MYTH

NOEL POLK

University Press of Mississippi / Jackson

Publication of this book is made possible in part by a grant from the University of Southern Mississippi.

"Upon Being Southernovelized" was first delivered at a conference in Bonn, Germany, and then published in the proceedings of that conference: Lothar Hönnighausen and Valeria Gennaro Lerda, eds., *Rewriting the South: History and Fiction*. Tübingen and Basel: Francke Verlag, 1993. "A Name for the City, A Shape for the Name" was first published in *The Journal of Mississippi History* 58(Spring 1996). "I Sonned a Father" originally appeared in the *Southern Review* (Spring 1983). All are reprinted here with the kind permission of editors and publishers.

Manufactured in the United States of America
00 99 98 97   4 3 2 1
The paper in this book meets the guidelines for permanence and durability of the Committee on Production Guidelines for Book Longevity of the Council on Library Resources.

Library of Congress Cataloging-in-Publication Data

Polk, Noel.
    Outside the southern myth / Noel Polk.
        p.   cm.
    ISBN 0-87805-979-2 (cloth : alk. paper).—ISBN 0-87805-980-6 (paper : alk. paper)
        1. Picayune (Miss.)—Social life and customs.   2. Polk, Noel—Homes and haunts—Mississippi—Picayune.   3. Southern States—Social life and customs.   I. Title.
    F349.P5P65   1997
    976.2'15—dc21   96-50045
                                                                            CIP

British Library Cataloging-in-Publication data available

FOR SCOTT, JENNIFER, MICHAEL

Listen, children:

Contents

Preface

The Southern Myth that I have lived outside of is that popular vision of the South that both controls and is controlled by the media: those various images that depict the entire South on the one hand as an ongoing national farce, a sort of charming caricature of itself—witness *The Dukes of Hazzard,* as if we are all creations of Al Capp—and on the other hand as a tragedy brought on by its own peculiar brand of pusillanimity, racism. Both hands are always completely aware of what the other is doing and often work together to oversimplify the South into one of two or three monoliths, as though all of the South were Natchez, Vicksburg, Selma, Little Rock, Jackson, Birmingham, and Oxford; as though every community had its own courthouse and Civil War memorabilia; as though every village were run by its own Will Varner or Big Daddy; as though every house were either a magnolia-laden white-columned antebellum mansion or a shotgun sharecropper shack. At worst, everybody brings up all the bad stuff whenever there's an opportunity. At best, we get "gritsed" to death whenever a southerner runs for president or does something else charming.

As a southern male, I almost invariably see myself depicted in the media as either a beer-drinking meanspirited pickup-driving redneck racist, a julep-sipping plantation-owning kindhearted benevolent racist, or, at best, a non-racist good ole boy, one of several variations of Forrest Gump, good-hearted and retarded, who makes his way in the modern world not because he is intelligent but because he's—well, good-hearted and retarded and simply doesn't know any better, qualities which in fact won't get anybody very far in any world I know outside of the Walt Disney studios of the fifties, various Jerry Lewis and Abbott and Costello movies, the Hollywood of *The Beverly Hillbillies*, or the Never-Never land of Mayberry. Indeed, sitcom formats like *The Andy Griffith Show* and *The Dukes of Hazzard* are in some ways even more offensive because in stressing the simple and simpleminded verities of these simple goodhearted small-town folk they also sanitize the South they depict by quietly eliding its racism and its black citizens. More serious shows, such as *Picket Fences*, which dealt sensitively with racial issues, tried to mainstream the South culturally by making its young hero a high school wrestler—a sport to my knowledge never associated with southern high schools or colleges. The image thus can't seem to adjust itself to the reality, no matter how hard it tries, no matter with what good intentions.

It's not only the popular media. During a recent presidential campaign, PBS's *McNeil-Lehrer News Hour* sent crews to different parts of the country to interview selected voters to try to get a fix on how the campaign seemed to be shaping up. They selected my friend and colleague, the historian Neil McMillen, to represent this area. In the course of the interview they shot film to give their viewers a sense of Hattiesburg, a visual context for Neil's interview. I don't know how other cities fared visually, but to depict Hattiesburg the PBS crew shot footage around the old train station and the less-affluent sections of town, to the complete exclusion of other, more prosperous, more middleclass, more mainstream America sections that might have presented Hattiesburg more completely as a reasonably cosmopolitan town that actually has hospitals, a university, shopping malls, extraordinary mansions, stock-brokers, and computer nerds. Instead, the crew opted for visuals that located Hattiesburg directly in the center of the South of the popular imagination—dirt and dirty streets, poor blacks and whites shuffling along—and they specifically evoked southern poverty. There are plenty of dirty streets, poverty, and shufflers, black and white, here, to be sure, but there are also plenty of those other, more prosperous and slightly less southern visuals that would have located Hattiesburg more nearly where it is in itself than where it exists as a "southern" place. My point is not to deny or sweep anything under the kudzu, but simply to point out the imbalance in the visual representation of the South in the national media, even when there's nothing of sensationalism to be gained.

I grew up in Picayune, Mississippi, a small city of just under 7,000, about fifty miles north of New Orleans, about the same distance south of Hattiesburg. Picayune is not antebellum, but it is indubitably southern. Like Hattiesburg, it is in the South but not of "The South." Picayune did not invest very much of its energies in *being southern* in any traditional sense; it was too busy trying to make itself urban and middleclass. It chopped steadily away at the rural world it had dragged itself out of and it would have run every pine tree in the Piney Woods through its saw and planing mills, if necessary, to separate itself from its rural origins: to keep the rural at a commodified distance, to make it a middleclass luxury instead of an economic necessity.

To appropriate Walker Percy's comment about his residence, Covington, Louisiana, Picayune was and is a "nonplace," an "interstice" in the South. Unlike towns of the southern myth, it was not a town or much of a community until well into the twentieth century. There were no Civil War battles in the area, so we had no statues of Civil War heroes adorning our courthouse square—we had no courthouse square, for that matter. We had no huge courthouse or antebellum homes sporting minié ball scars which we showed to visitors. I never to my knowledge talked to a Civil War veteran or anybody else who knew one, and I never heard tales about *The War*. Andrew Jackson and his troops marched through the area on the way to fight the battle of New Orleans, but that was in another war and so does not really count.

I was not surrounded by natural-born storytellers; I had only one uncle who fancied himself one, who would stumble through a joke and laugh himself into hysterics while repeating the punch line every time his audience's polite laughter subsided. I did not grow up imbibing from my mother's milk or from my ancestors an overwhelming sense of myself *as a southerner.* When I studied Mississippi and southern history in high school, I might as well have been studying the history of Afghanistan; I *still* cannot keep the names of Confederate and Union generals straight. Like Eudora Welty, I just *hate* and am bored by the South's obsession with the Civil War.

There was racism in Picayune, of course, but I am hard put to recall so much as a single act of overt bad manners between the races, though of course we all knew what the boundaries were. The air around me was not charged with racial tension, with religious perversion, with old maid sisters who made moonshine from an old family recipe, with scandal or gossip-mongering about sexually frustrated old maids, with a sense of the past, or with any of those small-town southern qualities so often represented to us in southern fiction and in the media. I seem to have grown up in a history-less backwash of the South, and my life as a southerner is completely out of kilter with the southern life portrayed in bad fiction and in the media.

The radical difference between my experience of the South and what all my reading and all the culture have told me "The South" was—and which has therefore defined me as a southerner—has over the past several years provided the grist for my intellectual and personal mills. My first grindings occurred in 1979 in an essay called "The Southern Literary Pieties," in which I tried to identify some of the forces in the Southern Literary Industry that had worked, especially since the late forties, to create a market for "southern" literature. This industry has its beginnings, of course, in the work of that influential group of scholars and poets, the Fugitives and the Agrarians, who gathered at Vanderbilt University in the first third of this century. Their agenda was, we are now beginning to understand (as perhaps, to be fair, they did not), politically charged and very defensive. At the industry's most political edge, it wanted to create a wall that would prevent northern social and economic encroachment and to forestall the changes they were sure that encroachment would bring. The wall was a melange of values that the industry claimed made the South, for all its notable economic and cultural shortcomings, *morally* superior to the North. "Southern" writers and critics thus promoted the worship of the rural and the natural as opposed to the urban and the technological; they valorized social and familial rootedness and opposed a disruptive mobility; they also connected literary quality with a peculiar and quasi-religious sense of geographical placeness.

It seems to me more likely that for the South these "values" were fallback positions—or, rather, what computer language now calls the default option: we made a virtue out of necessity. That is, rootedness, a fixation to a geographical "place," and a devotion to the rural were probably functions of southerners' financial limitations: we couldn't afford to move to California to get away from the rear end of the family mule or from the families that drove us crazy; otherwise we very well might have. Curiously—or not—nearly all of the Nashville Fugitive-Agrarian crowd, those who articulated the agrarian virtues so forcefully in their 1930 manifesto *I'll Take My Stand,* got out of the South, certainly out of their rural beginnings, just as soon as they possibly could, and began to sanitize and romanticize that rural world in their writing. No plows or outdoor toilets for these folks, no matter how desirable they were for other southerners, no matter how much moral "value" attached to them.

The CEOs and wannabe moguls of this industry thus defined "southern" literature as based in qualities that reified nature, rootedness, family, geography, and the tragic sense of history (a euphemism, I believe, for some more accurate phrase like "the niggers and the Yankees really played hell with us"): qualities through which they managed to sentimentalize and so soften the harsher edges of the South's history. They proscribed literature that did not valorize these things and applied the standards very rigidly: they properly revered William Faulkner and Eudora Welty as "southern" writers, but only so long as they wrote "southern" fiction. When writers presumed to step outside Mississippi, as Faulkner did in *A Fable* and Welty did in *The Bride of the Innisfallen*, critics concluded that they had committed gratuitous acts of literary suicide by cutting themselves free of their geographical tether. The "southernness" of "southern" writers, then, often became more impor-tant than the writing itself to these critics and readers, and what they believed was "southern" was mostly a reflection of their own backgrounds and values. Walker Percy spent a good deal of his humor denying that he was a "southern" writer; Cleanth Brooks wrote at least one essay to demonstrate that Percy was indeed a "southern" writer, no matter what he said.

No doubt my differences from these formidable critics are gener-ational. I am a pre-babyboomer, born during World War II; for most of my formative years I was stuck in the historical crack between the old guard and the new. I watched the fifties and the sixties from that historical crack, trying to deal with confusions and sympathies that ran both before and after me, hoping perhaps to shore up the old guard but not to get left behind by the new; I wanted to have it both ways. I now see that that crack was a kind of Maginot Line where I mostly buried myself in the bunker, hid from the action in the very act of positioning myself to fight off the enemy, whichever direction he came from and providing I could identify him in time.

But my differences are also intellectual and, perhaps, more personal than I care to admit. I will not argue that the South of the popular media has no basis in fact—my Lord, there're too many monuments and newsreels to be able to argue that. Nor will I engage the debate about whether there continues to be a real "South" in these days of McDonald's and Kmarts on every corner. What I do propose to illustrate in this little volume is that neither of those debates seems aware that there has *always* been another southern culture, one trying its best to work its way up to an identifiable, certifiable middleclass way of life, that has always engaged its own history and its received history in its own way, on its own terms, terms not all that different from those of middleclass American towns everywhere.

I grant, of course, that descriptions of the quotidian are not so interesting or dramatic as repeated stories about Bull Connor's German shepherds or Ross Barnett's or George Wallace's confrontation with those who would demand their civil rights. But such places as Picayune, which are far more numerous than the Selmas or Vicksburgs or Shilohs, often get defined out of the southern history that Selma and Natchez symbolize, and I want to claim in these pages a modest space somewhere on the historical and cultural maps for both the southernness and the mainstream By God American normality of my home town and others like it. I am weary to death of books and movies about how quaint and curious southerners are; my Picayune folks were normal Americans. Truly, it is possible for a southerner to love normality and even to be normal.

·   ·   ·

I have resisted the suggestion that I call these meditations "memoirs," partly because I'm just not old enough to have significant memories, and partly because I don't want to give to memory the sheen of privilege that presides like a nimbus over the word "memoir." I despise and repudiate the sentimentalization of memory and history that so frequently charges "southern" memoirs—indeed, a good deal of southern literature and life. I do not intend these essays as acts of aggression on my past, but neither do I intend them as warm—well, maybe some of them are; it *is* my life— memories of an "innocent" time when things were better than they are now, or of dramatic times when I learned about and heroically, through titanic struggle, rejected my southern heritage, or of fonder times when I ate Mom's biscuits by poking a hole in the edges and filling them with sorghum* molasses.

My days in Picayune were not innocent days—what does that mean, anyway? there never were any "innocent" days anywhere, I suspect—nor were they particularly "good" or "bad" days either. They were mostly generic days that happened like days everywhere else in America. My childhood in Picayune was by no means a "better" time than now, and I wouldn't live there again, relive my adolescence there (or anywhere else, of course: and there's the real nub of it all), for anything: as Tommy Stewart used to say of I. J. Smith's English class, I'd rather go to hell twice than have to live there again. But that, I ask my friends still in Picayune please to believe, is a statement about me and not about Picayune or about them. I can hardly think of a single person I knew there without a great deal of pleasure; they were for the most part gracious, open, mannersable, and completely accessible human beings, neither grotesque nor curious nor quaint, and not particularly "southern," either. I am certain that geography didn't give them, or me, any especial leg up as loving folks or as freaks.

Finally, I have trouble thinking of these essays as "memoirs" because they are mostly about things that *didn't* happen to me, things I didn't do or participate in, and in fact a good deal of this book is about things I don't remember. Also, I have forgotten a lot and am mostly happy to have done so. There is a blank spot right in the middle of where my memory ought to be, like the railroad yard that substitutes for Picayune's center. I actually think of these meditations as an "anti-memoir," and I would prefer not to be in these pages at all as a character or even as a consciousness, since I am not writing about me but about that part of

---

*Yes, I know folks pronounce it "sogrum" in many parts of the South. Not in Picayune.

the South that I grew up in. I am here inevitably, but only, I hope, to the extent that I was and am part of that part of that South and can only describe it as I saw it, from where I stood when I was looking at it, as modulated and refined by where I now stand thinking about it.

Two people are conspicuously, and deliberately, absent (mostly) from these pages: my mother and my brother, both very much alive and perfectly capable of having their own memories of these days, these people, that could be and probably are quite different from mine; they, after all, lived in Picayune longer than I did. I don't know how to write about them and I couldn't in any case speak for or about them in ways that would presume to describe their experiences in the same time and space that I grew up in. Though nearby at all times, they occupy a quite different place on my emotional map than my father does. Doubtless there is much here that they will remember differently, perhaps a good deal that will cause them pain, as it has caused me. I hope not, but if so I hope they will not take my memories as intentionally hurtful to them or to anybody else, because I love them very much. My memories are my own; they have a right to theirs too, a right not to be hurt by them. One of the most moving experiences of my early manhood occurred one afternoon when I watched my grandmother Hamilton weep uncontrollably while listening to Tennessee Ernie Ford sing "Precious Memories." She was a little embarrassed by her tears and laughed nervously when she saw that I had noticed her. I never asked whether she wept from pleasure or pain.

I thank Karolyn Wrightson, Gary Stringer, Charles Bolton, Lynn Gammill, Elisabeth Muhlenfeld, Charlie Newman, Joe Cooper, Jack Napier, Peggy Prenshaw, Lothar Hönnighausen, Peter Nicolaisen, John Dittmer, Robert Hamblin, Kenneth G. McCarty, Chrissie Wilson, Bridget Pieschel, Robyn Preston, and Seetha A-Srinivasan for reading and commenting on portions of this manuscript; Lynn McKnight did a fine job of copyediting. Gloria Norris worked extraordinarily hard in its behalf.

I am especially grateful to Jack T. Kirby, who read the entire manuscript and made many suggestions for improvement, and to Neil R. McMillen, for long discussions and much advice about its content. Jack and Neil have made my memories better than they would have been had I left myself to my own devices.

N.P.
Hattiesburg
September 1996

OUTSIDE
the
SOUTHERN
MYTH

Upon Being Southernovelized

MY TOWN, MY DEPARTMENT, MY FRIENDS,
AND ME IN A CARPETBAGGER NOVEL

When I was a lad at Boy Scout or church camp, I'd have to pose with the other campers for a group photo. There were lots of us; we would be lined up in three or four rows like a choir and we would stretch for ten to twenty yards in front of the camera. The camera used to take such a wide photograph was a curious creature that moved slowly from left to right, panning the group as it exposed only a portion of the film at a time, while inside the camera the film rolled from one spool to another in the opposite direction, so that everyone had to be extremely still while the camera's eye passed where we were. The resulting photograph was eight or nine inches high and sometimes as wide as two or three feet. If you were very fast, you could stand on the top row at one end, have your picture taken, then after the camera had rolled by jump down and race around behind the group, beat the camera to the other end, and have your picture taken there too; thus you'd appear twice in the same picture. I did this as often as I could claim space on both ends of the back row.

Are these photos accurate representations of my camping days? Well, manifestly, Yes; but just as manifestly No, since although they are demonstrably group photos, they do not readily yield and so cannot account for the activity *behind* the posed group that makes my double appearance possible. My double appearance is in fact available only to those who can interpret the photo correctly, and only those who are willing to examine the photograph closely, looking at the individual faces rather than at the group, can hope to see that the group photo is not exactly what it purports to be. It helps a great deal, interpreting these photographs, if you have some historical knowledge of or actual experience with such cameras.

I now know that a good deal of my pleasure in those group shots was in the knowledge that I had put one over on the photographer, on the chaperons, on the group, on posterity, and also on the camera itself, since by being literally in two places in the same photograph, I had signalled the photographer's activity in composing the picture in the first place—both the mechanics of the camera and the volatility of the object of the camera's eye, which can so easily subvert the camera and make of the photo both a truth and a lie. And thus I know that any group photo depends upon the complicity of the group.

I'd like to propose such group photos as metaphors for my life as a southerner, and to describe here not what it *means* but what it *feels like* to be a member of a group so frequently posed and photographed by scholars and by the media, and to discuss some of the strategies I as a southerner have used to keep from being rendered invisible by their various cameras. What I am going to describe may be similar to the experiences of others who find themselves being defined and delimited by presumptions about the group of which they are a part. Any time I say "Mississippian" or "southerner," you might well substitute "women" or "African American" or "Native American" or any other much-studied group.

There is a wonderful scene in Walker Percy's *The Moviegoer* in which Binx Bolling strolls through New Orleans' French Quarter hoping to get a glimpse of William Holden, who is in town to make a movie. Binx is not interested in Holden the movie star, but rather in the "heightened reality" that Holden *as* "movie star" represents. In the scene, Holden is being represented in a novel about (among other things, of course) the peculiar reality which reality attains only after being re-presented in some form which is different from the reality that is being re-presented and which, as in the case of Percy's Binx's Holden in Percy's Binx's French Quarter, cannot be denied or disregarded, not even momentarily, not even when one is confronted with the *real* reality of the person or place itself. (In the novel, we can speak not of the *real* reality of either Holden or the French Quarter, but only of their fictional reality.) Binx soon spots Holden, who is looking for a match. He asks a group of housewives from Hattiesburg, Mississippi—actually they are women who "look like housewives from Hattiesburg," about a hundred miles to the north of New Orleans—who become flustered at running so unexpectedly upon so "real" a person as Holden, and are therefore unable to supply him with something so mundane as a match. Holden then encounters a young man and woman for whom Binx creates a background as honeymooners from the Northeast. They of course recognize the actor and, in Binx's construction of the encounter, the young man pulls himself together and offers Holden a light so casually that in Binx's eyes he establishes his own reality in ways that the women like Hattiesburg housewives have forever forfeited their right to.

For Binx the meat of the episode lies in that young man, whom he and Percy have created and interpreted for us. I, however, who live in Hattiesburg, always stop short at the image of the women who "look like" housewives from Hattiesburg. Those of you who live in "places"—I use the term in Percy's sense of locations partaking of a definite historical reality that has been written down or photographed or otherwise "placed" in history and literature, places like New Orleans or Paris or Oxford or Bonn or Atlanta—may not even notice it anymore when your city, your place, figures in a movie or a work of fiction (though I'll bet that the closer a film or a book gets to naming or describing your particular neighborhood, street, or corner, the closer you come to taking particular notice), and you may not take it personally when a character in a novel is described as someone who "looks like" someone from the Bronx, the fifth arrondissement, or Los Angeles, or as someone who "looks like" a college professor.

But I confess I do notice this passage for a number of reasons, not the least of which is the fact that the reference to Hattiesburg makes *The Moviegoer* a wonderful novel to teach to students *in Hattiesburg*; it provides a built-in illustration of Binx's doctrine of certification, which emerges precisely from that peculiar sense of reality that movies and photographs and, need I say it, fiction, give to the world, especially to the portions of the world we live in or visit and which we can therefore experience both actually and imaginatively, through our own and someone else's focussing eye. For Binx, to see your own place on the screen is to render it real, certified:

> Nowadays when a person lives somewhere, in a neighborhood, the place is not certified for him. More than likely he will live there sadly and the emptiness which is inside him will expand until it evacuates the entire neighborhood. But if he sees a movie which shows his very neighborhood, it becomes possible for him to live, for a time at least, as a person who is Somewhere and not Anywhere.

Why, I ask my students, does Binx/Percy choose Hattiesburg? What revelation about Hattiesburg, this real place we live in, are we startled into by its sudden eruption in a work of fiction? Does it make us feel more "real," more "placed" to see ourselves evoked in a work of fiction? What does it mean that Binx describes the women as *like* housewives from Hattiesburg? What are housewives from Hattiesburg like? What does it say about us who live in Hattiesburg and so form the collective model of Hattiesburg-ness to which those women are being compared? What is the *essence of Hattiesburg-ness?*

Something vaguely snide in Binx's tone insinuates something suspect about Hattiesburg, and even if I am being intolerably defensive and making more of it than can possibly be made, the reference still seems to cast a pall of existential blandness around Hattiesburg. In fact, Hattiesburg is pretty much what Percy called his home, Covington, Louisiana, a "non-place," which in *The Moviegoer* is suddenly catapulted into place-ness by virtue of its representation as the epitome of non-placeness, of "nowhereness." Though it is in the South, it becomes in the novel a sort of black hole of middleclass normality, devoid of any historical sense of "place" that informs New Orleans and especially the French Quarter, and lacking the kind of history or character that confers "place" on a location. The reference is a casual one, almost a throwaway (and perhaps the more powerful for that), and although we know that Percy himself wasn't all that enamored of "place"—places get "used up," he once wrote—and chose to live in Covington precisely because it *was* a non-place, a sort of "interstice" in the South; and although Binx himself eschews the "placeness" of New Orleans and the French Quarter and his aunt's storied Garden District to live in the middle- and working-class nonplace of Gentilly, a New Orleans suburb at the Lake Pontchartrain end of Elysian Fields Avenue, the other end of which meets the Mississippi River in the French Quarter; although we know all this, I say, we Hattiesburg readers can't help but take umbrage at the reference: why didn't he pick *Covington* as his example, for crying out loud? Why pick on us? After all, Hattiesburg is a university town, filled with lots of very sophisticated people who can spell Nietzsche and Kierkegaard and who infinitely prefer *Die Grosse Fuge* as the proper final movement of Beethoven's Opus 130 to the movement he replaced it with; citizens in Hattiesburg stand around on street corners comparing Schopenhauer and Heidegger, and housewives discuss quantum physics at beauty parlors. But neither our umbrage nor our indisputable claims of how *wrong* or at least problematic the reference is can displace the fact that somehow, at some point in time, for reasons unfathomable, Hattiesburg, *my* burg, became, for Percy, the very model for cultural nowhereness—placelessness and historylessness— and I am forever tarred with that cultural brush.

Thus Hattiesburg becomes a significant if minor point of reference in *The Moviegoer*; it is a southern site raised to its highest level of placeness by a work of fiction which offers it up as a non-place, as partaking of no past that would give it purchase on some identity other than its own. Hattiesburg is southern geographically, but it is not antebellum, it is not rural, it is not "small," and its population is heavily professional and urban. It too is an interstice in the "South" and therefore does not have much purchase on "southern" history, since apparently almost nothing of any *fictional* significance that happened to "The South" happened also to Hattiesburg.

In fact, that is not completely true. I can point to plenty of racial turmoil in the fifties and sixties—some murders, at least one racial rape, some bombings—to give Hattiesburg its own reasonable claim on "southern history." But I find myself asserting that claim here with a perverse sort of actual pride, which is purely outrageous. As a southerner I somehow have to attach myself to an interesting history, even, perhaps especially, if it's a troubling or wicked history, rather than admit to a boring or a merely local one, since of course a tragic sense of history is one burden all southerners have to have in order to *be southern.* Given the Birminghams, the Selmas, the Jacksons, the Memphises, the Philadelphias and McCombs, Hattiesburg's claim is a small one; and, in any case, we've produced no bard interested enough to locate, much less to chronicle, our burden of guilt and all those other things we as southerners hold dear, no matter if we in Hattiesburg have to share New Orleans's or Atlanta's or Birmingham's or Oxford's, no matter if we have to reach the 150 miles into the Mississippi Delta and to Natchez to appropriate our necessary share of the South's plantation heritage.

But though we have been fictionally certified in terms of our blandness, as a city in "The South" Hattiesburg nevertheless shares in a form of certification that imposes on it all of the opprobrium, and none of the pleasures, generated by Mississippi's and the South's historical image as backward, racist, poor, ignorant, violent, exotic: above all, *different.* As a southerner, I gather that I myself exude these things, like an odor, when I travel outside the South; this is baggage that I as southerner am expected to have, and I am still confronted by intelligent people who, if they know me as a reasonably intelligent and sophisticated person before they find out I'm from Mississippi and live there by choice, always find ways to sympathize with me; if they learn where I live before they get to know me, it's often quite difficult to get past that geographical and psychological fact. Do not tell me that this "odor" is a product of my imagination, that I am too defensive about my southernness for my own good, though doubtless that is true enough. I have talked to too many northern scholars who don't want to take a job at my university because they have just seen *Mississippi Burning,* and I know too many northerners who have taken jobs in Mississippi, to the consternation and even befuddlement of their northern friends, and report that since becoming Mississippians, their experience is the same as mine. And I've heard Ed Koch, then mayor of perhaps the most racially troubled city in North America, say that the incident in Bensonhurst was the kind of thing that happens in Mississippi, not in New York.

Thus the "burden" of southern history for me as a southerner is that though personally I live outside of it and do not partake of it I am nevertheless quite often defined by it. Though I am not *in* southern history, I am indubitably *of* it, have been certified by it: I bear a reality that is imposed on me by the group photo. Being in a film or a novel, or in this case a version of history, may indeed cause one's "certification," and it may be that the citizens of Oxford and of Mississippi felt "certified" through their collective appearance in Faulkner's fiction, but I'd bet they did not. And so I believe that Binx is wrong. I believe that photography really does steal the souls of people and places and that being photographed or novelized renders one less real rather than more. I believe that "place" is always a group photo and that "place" is always *somewhere else*, since I have talked to bored employees at the top of the French Alps who wanted to go to Mississippi. This I believe.

As a southerner, I look into the mirrors of southern history and fiction and do not see much that has any direct relation to my life as a southerner. I do not in fact see my self or even a self that I think I am but some reconstruction of a self that I am told I am, or ought to be, by virtue of being southern. Thus I am, like William Holden in *The Moviegoer*, a trope for myself, and I more often feel canceled than certified: eyes looking into eyes looking into eyes, in an infinite baffle of resonances and myths whose sources are no longer locatable, least of all by me, if there is a me to be found somewhere between "southern history" and Hattiesburg-ness. I as southerner stand between two mirrors so huge that they reflect nothing but each other and I can see nothing that is not reflected in them; before and behind me multiple simultaneous replications of my image speed away into infinity, and no matter how I strain to one side, trying to get even a fleeting glimpse of the original, singly-, simply-reflected *I*, I cannot ever see it. I am forever blocked by the image facing me from the mirror, no matter which mirror I face.

Even as I grew up halfway between Hattiesburg and New Orleans, so do I now live, as a southerner, somewhere between the actuality and the cultural re-presentation of that actuality, and it's often very difficult to distinguish between the two—if there is a distinction. As Percy's mad Lancelot puts it, "Looking at oneself in a mirror is a self-canceling phenomenon. Eyes looking into eyes make a hole which spreads out and renders one invisible." I am taken for a character in *The Dukes of Hazzard* but I'm really a character in *The Sot-Weed Factor*.

After some years of thinking about these things in the abstract, I was given reason to think about them in the concrete a couple of years ago when James Kaplan published his first novel, *Pearl's Progress* (1989), a *roman à clef* about his year as a member of the University of Southern Mississippi English Department in the late seventies. You may imagine our interest and concern when we heard about Jim's novel, and you may, if you like, also imagine that I approached the book with some trepidation, wondering how accurately Kaplan had reported on my colleagues and whether I myself had made the cut: whether I had made enough of an impression to have made it into the book, and whether *I* would be both recognizable and, well, as *likeable* and *charming* as in my heart of hearts I know myself to be. I greeted with a combination of relief and irritation the fact that though there is a departmental Faulknerian at Kaplan's fictional Pickett State University, a decidedly minor character, he is *not at all like me.* Kaplan nails many of my colleagues, past and present, very accurately, with a wonderful replication of language and gesture that make them recognizable, but he missed me completely.

The departmental "Faulknerian" at Pickett State is described on the book's dust jacket as "baby-faced Perry Armbruster, capable of working a reference to 'ol' Mr. Bill Faulkner' into any conversation." In one scene in the novel, Kaplan describes Armbruster as he talks about "ol' Mr. Bill's" drinking habits, "his large brown eyes wide and reverent behind brown-rimmed horn glasses. In fact, everything about Perry—eyes, glasses, hair, three-piece suit; the Mr. Pibb root beer in his hand—seemed brown. Faulkner was being wheeled out like a statue on a wagon"; during a scene at Armbruster's house, a reception for a visiting poet, in town for a reading at Pickett State, Perry is visibly elated at the success of his party:

"Perry, apple cheeks aglow, could scarcely have been prouder if his dear dead Faulkner had dropped down from heaven for a bourbon."

Of course Perry Armbruster is not "me": I own but hardly ever wear three-piece suits, nor horn-rimmed glasses; I was not then, any more than now, "baby-faced" or "apple-cheeked," and I'd rather drink water from the lower Hudson than a Mr. Pibb. But Perry is married to a woman named Patty, as I was, and the reception for the visiting poet is one I well remember—or think I do: the visiting poet reads a piece very much like a story John Barth read when *he* visited USM; Patty and I hosted a reception not for John Barth but for Doris Betts, but if Betts behaved at our house the way Kaplan's poet behaves at Perry's, I'm not aware of it.

Perry Armbruster is a pretty straightforward denizen of Hattiesburg, an apotheosis of Hattiesburg-ness, to use a Faulknerian word Perry would doubtless appreciate. Kaplan presents him as a very minor character, a doting and perhaps slightly dotty, but harmless enough Faulknerian (perhaps now de rigueur in English Departments, especially in the South), and he is a curious combination of Hattiesburg-ness and southernness: he wears a three-piece suit and talks about "ol' Mr. Bill"—words which *God knows* have never issued from my mouth. Kaplan transcribes this locution as *ol'*—not o-l-d—Mr. Bill, to give some flavor of a southern dialect to Perry's language that is somehow at odds with his three-piece suit, and so makes either the three-piece suit or the dialect an Armbruster pose: he is either a good ol' boy aspiring to three-piece intellectual suitdom or he has come from three-piece suit stock and is faking the good ol' boy, as Faulkner's Gavin Stevens does, in order to put on this northerner who *by god wants and expects southern.*

It is impossible to know from the novel whether Perry Armbruster is putting Pearl on and, if so, whether Philip Pearl knows it or not— whether Kaplan knows whether he was being put on or not. I do not know whether he is satirizing me or bardolatry, especially the really virulent strain of it in southern literary studies; I do not know whether Kaplan saw me then as, or whether I really was then or am now, such a bardolater—indeed, I do not know whether I was then, or am now, such a vacuous, if harmless, creature as Armbruster. I cannot figure out how much of his portrait is of me as "southerner," how much of me as apotheosis of Hattiesburg-ness. But no matter: in Perry Armbruster I am not certified, but bifurcated, deconstructed, pulled apart by a self-canceling vision of myself in that mirror, even if Kaplan didn't have me in mind at all when he created Armbruster.

On the other hand, if Kaplan is satirizing me, it may well be—I don't really remember—I *hope*—that he is satirizing a me that was putting him on, since I can play the good ol' boy if I choose. As Doris Betts has written of southerners in general, I can *do southern*: I can supply it upon demand or expectation for those who think they want it. I can give you what I think you think you want, and I do so partly because it's fun to put you on, but also partly because it's often easier to give you what you want than to expect you to accept something other than what you are going to see no matter what you are looking at. I can hunker for hours, eat grits by the gallon, drive a pickup, talk with a twang and a drawl, but I draw the line at chewing tobacco or dipping snuff; I own three Patsy Cline and a dozen Willie Nelson albums and mostly sing Hank Williams, Sr., in the shower. I can fry catfish and hushpuppies and drink large quantities of Dixie or any other kind of beer while doing so, and the clerk in my local liquor store used to be a guy named Billy Bob who once sold me a bottle of what he called *pie-not nawer* wine. I can preach you a sermon that'll make you want to be a Southern Baptist and make your mama and papa want to send me their social security checks every month. I can do Rhett to your Scarlett and, given enough time and incentive, Scarlett to your Rhett. But I also drink St. Emilion and eat Beluga caviar. If forced to choose I would listen to Kiri Te Kanawa and Elisabeth Schwarzkopf rather than Patsy Cline and K. D. Lang. On good days I too can spell Nietzsche and Kierkegaard and would drive a Porsche if I could afford one. I do not come from a slaveholding family; nobody that I know of in my ancestry was a Confederate soldier and I still do not know all the names of the Confederate generals. I have no uncles or aunts or neighbors who are natural born storytellers. My history is more pathetic than tragic, and the things I feel guilty about are none of your damned business. So be careful when you try to assemble southerners for the group photo, because I will be in at least two different places and running like hell behind the group to bollix up your artfully arranged pose.

All this would be a real problem if I took it more seriously than I do, if *Pearl's Progress* had become a more prominent novel, if Kaplan's satire were more vicious, or if my colleagues and I were sufficiently prominent that the portrait would excite more attention in the media. But the problem doesn't really immobilize me: it is, after all, only a problem of history and fiction, and I can have some fun with it. Of course this essay is itself partly fiction, another form of that mirror for which I have constructed a fictional self which can be canceled. I do not in fact go around all day feeling canceled or even diminished by being southern. For my purposes here, I must dramatize my lack of a claim on southern history and experience as a problem, a neurosis even, but in fact it is much more an intellectual problem than a social one, and it erupts socially only when I am confronted by folks who presume to see me as a blur somewhere in the group photo, at which point I become, for them and perhaps even for me, a mirror of some southern actuality that I may be only performing for them. I start puttin' on ol' massa, a massa who needs puttin' on precisely because he's too stupid and rude to know he's being put on. The young honeymooner in *The Moviegoer* establishes his own reality by pretending to ignore Holden's heightened reality. Holden does the same thing: he pretends to ignore such assaults on his reality as the women like Hattiesburg housewives make. Ignoring the mirror may be the only line of defense for people who are tropes for themselves.

James Kaplan—not a southerner but a carpetbagger, like his protagonist Philip Pearl a New York Jew (itself a frequently posed and photographed group)—has made a serious effort to rewrite the South. *Pearl's Progress* is precisely about Pearl's reconciliation of the national image of Mississippi with the reality of his experience of it. And although his adventures include many traditionally "southern" images and characters, Pearl's "Progress" is measured by his growing refusal to allow the image, the mirror, to control what he sees. Pearl arrives in Mississippi preternaturally conscious of Goodman, Schwerner, and Cheney, murdered barely fifteen years before, and of how alien he and "The South" are to each other. He expects to find Mississippi as "[d]ark, mysterious, deeply poor. Faulknerian. It was shameful, he knew, but the tourist in Pearl had expected black children playing in mud puddles in dirt streets." A fine edge of realism in Kaplan will not let him, even this early in the novel, overlook the reality, and he notes, unsentimentally, that he *would* see black children playing in mud puddles in dirt streets later, during a frantic drive to the Delta.

In Pickett Pearl finds some worthy and wonderfully drawn "southern" characters, but he also discovers that the English Department chairman is named Marschak, the director of the Creative Writing Program is named Wunsch, the large department store in town is Goldblum's; he is treated in the emergency room of the hospital by an Indian doctor named Gupta, and even his postman is from Modesto, California; the woman he chases throughout the novel is Francesca Raffi, daughter of Giovanni, a composer and member of the Pickett State Music Department who drives an Alfa Romeo around the Mississippi countryside and acts a good deal like a mafia don: these are all, need I say, wonderfully accurate portraits of my colleagues, whom Kaplan nails, while of course missing me completely. The best characterization in the novel is one of the departmental poets, Ted Juniper, a beer-drinking pot-smoking pickup-driving good ol' boy par excellence, who can play and sing country music, who can quote equal amounts of Roethke, Doughty, and Davy Crockett and who, Pearl discovers, has a sophisticated and well-read and -annotated library of poetry and criticism better than his own. In short, Pearl comes prepared to find a miasmal Faulknerian Mississippi; what he finds is that Mississippi is, quite simply, like "every place else." This is hardly an epiphany of any power or magnificence, but my experience of outsiders coming to Hattiesburg and to the South is that they are *still* startled by such revelations.

Walker Percy spent a good part of his literary energies questioning assumptions about southernness; he wittily rejected numerous accusations that he was a "southern" writer and tried to rewrite, reinscribe, a South that had become invisible even to itself through its, and the nation's, preoccupation with its image. Percy managed to get around the image in the mirror and I believe actually saw what he was looking at. His South, like Barry Hannah's, is a South rewritten partly through his overt rejection of southern images, partly through an outright attack on them. I suspect that there is more than a little of Percy's own hatred of the controlling southern images in his Lancelot who, himself of fallen Louisiana gentry, driven mad by the fact that his nouveau-riche Texas wife is not only sleeping with a Hollywood director but is also helping him build movie sets that will more accurately "reflect" the South on the screen than will the actual South they are living in. Driven mad by this, he strikes the match that blows them all up: unfaithful wife, unfaithful filmmakers, unfaithful history and fiction, restored and modernized antebellum mansion: blown to bits.

Percy may share Lance's madness and malice on this score. I know I do. Maybe what drives Lance mad is the knowledge that the South can't really be rewritten by a southerner. Maybe only a New York Jew can rewrite it. A southerner has to erase it first and start over from scratch. I don't hate it, I don't, I don't; but I keep looking for a match and can't find one in Hattiesburg.

A Name for the City,
A Shape for the Name

AN ANTI-SOUTHERN HISTORY

SOUTHERN HISTORY

Picayune has no center, really—geographical, historical, or metaphorical. It was incorporated into a village, and then into a town just after the turn of the century and named after the leading New Orleans newspaper of the day, the *Daily Picayune*. Apparently, though not certainly, Eliza Jane Poitevent Nicholson, the editor of the *Picayune*, gave the name to a railroad stop called Bailey's Switch in the mid-1880s when the New Orleans & Northeastern Railway laid its tracks. She had grown up in the area, and as owner and editor of the *Daily Picayune* she had agitated editorially about the direction the railroad line north from New Orleans would take. No one has suggested anything untoward or self-interested in this, but it pleases me to think that her investment in the railroad's path was directly related to her need for ironhorse transportation from New Orleans to her Mississippi home. Of course she didn't want the tracks running *through* her property or even close enough for her to hear the whistle or have to put up with the other turmoil and clutter of people and businesses that railroads bring with them—she had all that in New Orleans—so the tracks run about two miles west of her home on the banks of the Hobolochitto, The Hermitage, the only antebellum house in the Picayune area. Apparently, though again not certainly, because she did so much to get the railroad for the area, she was given (it is not clear by whom) the privilege of naming the station. She had already given her married name, Nicholson, to the railroad stop two or three miles south of Picayune, and I can only presume there was a reason she did not give Picayune one of her other names but instead offered the name of her newspaper. In any case, the area had been named Picayune or, for some reason, *Pickayune*, for about two decades before its incorporation as a village; it could just as easily have been named Poitevent, or even Eliza Jane.

Picayune: the price of her daily paper, a small Spanish coin, half of a bit, 6¼¢. The Spanish word derives from the French *picaillon*, an ancient coin worth something less than a *centime.** A picayune has always been used to buy something low in cost hence low in value; it thus designates something cheap and/or trivial and as an adjective means pettiness and even pusillanimity: picayunish. It would be hard to imagine a town name less idealistic, less romantic, less *interesting* in its origins, than Picayune. It genuflects to no founding or important family or political figure (Crosby, Hattiesburg, Poplarville, Jackson); it pays no homage to settlers' Eastern or European ancestries (Oxford, New Orleans, Columbia, Monticello), to local Indian antecedents (Natchez, Biloxi, Pascagoula), or to local geographical features (Brookhaven, Gulfport, D'Lo [originally *de l'eau*], Ocean Springs, Pearl River, Walkiah Bluff); it involves no normal and natural allegiance to an economic base (Logtown, Kiln, Lumberton), and it maintains no witty dialogue with its own history (Hot Coffee, Bailey's Switch). That is, it recognizes, celebrates, *claims*, nothing inherently or historically its own.

---

*There are some slightly variant versions of the word's etymology; given here is the version I grew up with.

You could easily make too much of the choice of the name, but it would certainly be wrong, for my purposes, to make too little: after all, *somebody* proposed it and others approved it, or at least went along with it, in ignorance of or actual contempt for the kinds of symbolic values we southerners are reputed to associate with naming. There would thus seem to be no magic in naming, since Picayune didn't suffer particularly from being so curiously named (quite the contrary, I'd say: but of course we will never know whether a different name might have created a different town), except for an occasional social discomfiture or awkwardness when, on band trips or at Scout camp, we would find ourselves called upon to explain the name. Our name's very oddness seemed to draw attention to itself, to force its lack of significance on others. Like a nondescript guest at a party whose very nondescriptness seems to augur some fascinating story if you could only draw it out but doesn't, Picayune insists upon the question, but can't supply the answer: it implies a significance it does not have.

Trips out of town, or entertaining visitors, became a lowgrade series not so much of humiliations as of reminders of that oddness. But even so it was not odd enough to work *for* me when I would try to explain, because the name contained no narrative hook that I could make into a story, nor even a peculiarity or quirk that I could turn into a joke:

"What kind of name is that?" someone would say.

"It's a small Spanish coin. Half a bit."

"Oh."

"A bit's half a quarter. Like two bits. You know: 'Shave and a haircut, six bits.'"

"Oh."

The name would thus lie flat and lifeless between us, too curious to leave alone and not interesting enough to fuel even a brief exchange, much less a conversation. So we would shuffle, not even uncomfortably, for less than a moment, and then find something else to talk about.

The name became especially dispiriting when somebody would make a connection with a brutally harsh cigarette packaged under the brand name Picayune.

"What kind of name is that?"

"It's a small Spanish coin. Half of a bit, like 'Shave and a h—' "

"Named for the cigarette?"

"No. For the newspaper."

"Oh."

All this "explaining" becomes even odder to me as I recall it now, since I do not remember ever asking anyone, or even hearing anybody else ask anyone, from Greenville, McComb or D'Lo, Crystal Springs, or Jackson to explain *their* town names.

"Picayune" means only what it names: money: and not even imaginative or grandiose amounts of it—not a quarter or a dollar or ten dollars or a hundred but rather the lowest possible, the least ambitious and empowering denomination of it and, more, a denomination named from two foreign and hence alien economies. I would like to believe that some wit went in to the name's selection, but I can't find the evidence to. If the name pays homage to Madame Nicholson's newspaper, I'm stuck with a symbolic homage to the current: not particularly even the new but simply the daily, the moment. If there is homage at all in the name, it is paid very indirectly to the logging and sawmill mindset of the original settlers, if not of the founders, who cut timber and moved on to where the trees were still growing.

I don't mean that Picayune's namers opted out of history or that if they had done so the town would have necessarily been better or worse off than Oxford, say, since one might argue that such places as Oxford can get mired in their own history—places get "used up," Walker Percy once wrote—and that such as Picayune, in taking an anti-historical and anti-symbolical stance in its name might well be understood as opting for a new world order, a twentieth-century order, a world open to possibilities that a slavish homage to founding families and ancestors and other such traditions can deny.

I don't for a moment think this is the case, even if such a case would fit my own arguments about the "other" South, the one different from that of the public mythology. But it is hard to escape a sense that the *geist*, at any rate, if not the actual namers, saw Picayune as temporary: that it sprang up mushroomlike along the railroad, clinging to it not even tenaciously, to serve the specific momentary comforts and needs of north-south transients, those coming through for a moment, a day, a year, long enough to eat a meal, spend the night, log a forest. Its one hold on permanence may well have been its fortunate location on the railroad rather than on the Pearl River, where logging ports like Jackson's Landing, Gainesville, Walkiah Bluff, Favre's Landing, Logtown, and Pearl River itself all faded when the railroad replaced the river as the principal route for commercial transport. The town namers even named its first streets—Haugh, Curran, and Harvey—for railroad officials, not for local residents. During the late fifties, my high school years, Picayune was awash first with the rumors about the NASA facility at Gainesville, where rocket engines were to be tested, and then, in the sixties, with the reality of the new folks, scientists and engineers from everywhere across the country, who lived in Picayune to work at NASA. In just under sixty years, then, Picayune changed from a halting-place for railroad travellers passing through on their way from New Orleans to Hattiesburg or Chicago or Washington, D.C., to a temporary residence for outlanders trying to get to the moon. It was ever a place for folks on their way somewhere else, or trying to help other folks get there.

If the namers intended an honorific, a totemic, connection with New Orleans, that, too, I'm afraid, testifies to Picayune's location in a historical and cultural and even metaphorical warp. The microscopic rural protestant mushroom of a railroad stop attached itself to a sprawling urban hothouse orchid of a richly historical and Catholic, foreign, even exotic, environment that is historically, psychologically, and culturally alien, perhaps even appalling to many or most of the settlers. The railroad's track was therefore not so much an umbilical cord through which nourishment flowed as, say, a spider's skein on which Picayune, dependant, hung. At some point Picayune named its central east-west thoroughfare Canal Street, after New Orleans' grander world famous promenade, while its own un-aptly named Main Street was and remains a decidedly minor little street running parallel to the railroad and intersecting Canal Street just west of the tracks.

Picayune thus cut its spiritual and metaphorical ties with its own political center in Jackson and attached itself not to a rising star of its own dreams and hopes, nor even to an energizing moment in its past, but in fact to its own opposite, its own moral and spiritual underbelly: New Orleans: a city, a mindset symbolizing all the things Picayune's protestant rhetoric claimed not to believe in. Clearly it was clinging to something it didn't want to give up no matter how protestant and rural and pious it forced itself to believe it actually was. Such a psychic split should have made for a more interesting history than it did.

A lot of this split is geographical, of course, since even before the interstate Picayune was slightly more than an hour away from New Orleans and nearly 3½ hours from Jackson. The interstate through the Honey Island Swamp put New Orleans barely 45 minutes away and left Jackson a still-formidable 2½ hours distant. By the time I left for college in 1961 Picayune had become a bedroom community for lots of folks who worked in New Orleans but preferred small-town life. Picayune still reads New Orleans newspapers, watches New Orleans television stations, listens to New Orleans radio, shops in New Orleans stores, goes to New Orleans theatre and movies and symphony and ballet, parties in its French Quarter, keeps up (willy-nilly) with New Orleans and Louisiana politics and sports, takes advantage of its economy by commuting there to work, disapproves of its crime, its political corruption, its casual morality. I never read a Jackson newspaper with any regularity until I left and I can't swear that I ever saw a *Clarion-Ledger* or *Daily News* until 1956 or 1957, when I began going with the Picayune band to State Band Contest in Jackson every spring. This was, of course, a mixed blessing.

i i .

Further, Picayune seems to exist on the one site in all of south Mississippi where nothing colorfully "historic" happened. Within an arc of sixty miles to the south and west, toward New Orleans and the Gulf Coast, lie places named Gainesville, Pearlington, Pearl River, Logtown, Santa Rosa, Caesar, Pool's Bluff, Napoleon, and Turtleskin, where people and things had been happening for centuries before Picayune and which are aptly named for those defining people and moments. South and west of Picayune, into Louisiana, lie the swamps of the Honey Island, a huge island in the middle of the Pearl River, which in the mid nineteenth century harbored the locally notorious Copeland gang, who may or may not have buried treasure there, and a prominent and successful New Orleans businessman, a Scot named Kirk MacCullough who sailed Lake Borgne and the bayous of the Pearl River delta under the *nom de pirate* of Pierre Rameau; other, lesser, pirates and rogues also roamed the area, and during the occupation of New Orleans Union gunboats patrolled the same waters. The Pearl River was generally alive with lumbermen and adventurers who with perhaps a larger stage for their exploits or even just more imagination and energy might have been worthy of their contemporaries if not peers on the Mississippi River and the Natchez Trace. Andrew Jackson and his army camped just east of Picayune at Caesar, on their way to fight the battle of New Orleans; Napoleon is so named because the exiled emperor's brother Jerome camped for a time on the banks of the Pearl while hatching a plot to raise support in

New Orleans to free the emperor from Helena; Choctaws had villages on the banks of the Hobolochitto in Picayune's northwest quadrant, its northern perimeter, and up and down the Pearl: they may have massacred some white settlers about the middle of the eighteenth century. All in all, it's not a bad assortment of characters and events, though character and event get more dense and interesting the closer they get to the Gulf Coast and New Orleans, where the money was. The upriver areas of south Mississippi merely got some of the spillover, as though character and event, like the river, had to back up occasionally when New Orleans and the coast reached even their astonishing limit.

But these Lower Pearl places seem extraordinary, dynamic, only by comparison with Picayune. In fact their histories are also, like Picayune's, mostly driven by fairly mundane economics and people, not by colorful characters or land- or cattle-barons or wars, massacres, swindles or frauds or gambles, not even racial animosities or agitations. What gangsterism, what organized violence and crime there was was not the fabulous turmoil of the Natchez Trace and Mississippi River bandits, doubtless at least partly because the stakes were much smaller and they'd have had to rob or murder their poor hardworking friends rather than wealthy strangers travelling through. The River and the Trace have been imaginatively defined by the fabulousness of their plantation economies and their underworld rogues—the Harpes, Hares, Mike Finks, and Murrells; the Pearl River valley equivalents, the members of the Copeland gang, say, were local thugs and thieves no matter how you cut it. They are minor and predictable, generic aberrations in a generic landscape, and they have almost no claim on the collective imagination even of the region, much less beyond it: Copeland "lore" is mostly a scholarly enterprise and even that limited to a recent reprint of Copeland's *Memoirs*, with a scholarly introduction.

There were no Civil War battles in the region and except for one company out of Gainesville only occasional stories of local volunteers for the Confederate army, going off to fight or returning home. Reconstruction didn't much affect the dailiness of the area's residents. Because the economy was not based in the plantation system—the soil did not permit farming on such a huge scale—there were not very many slaves before the war; thus after the War and Reconstruction, the economy did not evolve into the monstrously exploitative sharecropper system that defined the social and economic structures of the Mississippi Delta and other plantation regions. Most workers, black and white, did after the war what they did before it: cut timber. Although to be sure there were racial problems connected with the pecking order among white and black millmen, there did not develop in the area the bitter and intense race relations that defined areas where sharecropping defined economic life. Like folks everywhere else, black and white people in the lower Pearl River basin mostly worked hard: the minor squabblings, the after-hours brawling, the personal turbulence, was mostly the normal and even ritualized steam-letting of normal folks otherwise engaged in the not particularly heroic act of survival.

Thus with very few exceptions south Mississippi's history is almost completely generic and probably not significantly different from other places with similar economies based in similar geographies. S. G. Thigpen Sr.'s several compilations of stories of the region's people and places testify, in spite of themselves, to the serious *dailiness* of settlers' lives and times.* His books are not history in the sense that they tell *a* story of the region, a story that has an organizing principle or focus, even if that focus were either simultaneity or chronology. They tell hundreds of little stories that bear a sort of random relation to each other: indeed,

---

Old Days and Old Ways (New York: Vantage, 1975); the others were published privately in Picayune, by Thigpen: *Next Door to Heaven* (1965); *Pearl River: Highway to Glory Land* (1965); *A Boy in Rural Mississippi* (1966); *Work and Play in Grandpa's Day* (1969).

the stories seem ordered more or less as they came to Thigpen, and what they most have in common are their similarities, their repetitiousness with only minor variations from one teller to another, and their inclusion in Thigpen's books. As "local histories" do, they record what people in Pearlington, say, wore, what stores sold and how much things cost, how people courted, worshipped, played, fought; how syrup was made; what it was like to deal with oxen; bathing on Saturday nights; how different things were then than now (i.e., how much better things were then). All these stories are interesting enough in themselves, of course, but none is peculiarly southern or even, I suspect, peculiar to the region; all of them could have been and doubtless have been told time and time again about other parts of the country.

Even so, less "happened" in Picayune than anywhere else in the region, even granting its more recent appearance on the stage of history. Thus in its oddness, Picayune's name posits a kind of metaphorical emptiness of event at and as its center; Picayune is a sort of vacuum around which the area's various political and geographical features and its history move in random elliptical orbits, without any particular causal relationships to it or to each other, like the randomly recorded recollections in Thigpen's books. This is all the more curious since Picayune, once established as the region's economic center, all but completely absorbed the older and comparatively more "historical" communities of the region, as though all those places with history were more than eager to allow themselves to be drained in to Picayune's historical vacuum. Economically the motion toward Picayune is perfectly understandable. When logging along the Pearl seriously diminished, the river towns, with no other economy to keep them going, had nothing but history to justify their continued existence and that wasn't enough: nothing symbolizes this better than the razing of Gainesville, Logtown, and Turtleskin by the U. S. government in order to make room for the NASA facility. The citizens of these towns had long done their business in Picayune; after the razing, many of them moved there with their money and their memories. Metaphorically, however, the folks who moved to and looked to Picayune did so precisely to escape history. Conveniently located in space, it was also conveniently located in time—conveniently insulated, that is, from the rush and roar of the chaotic flow of "event" that pulled the historical rug out from under the older sites.

I do not mean that Picayune has no history of its own; of course it does.* It just cannot point to a galvanizing moment, actual or mytho-logical, that shaped its future, defined its character, or otherwise gave it some claim upon the imagination—the razing of (or the refusal to raze) a square or a courthouse by invading armies, a lynching, a plantation tradition, a duel, a battle—though the commercial establishment there did in fact try (desperate, but completely predictable) to claim its place as a star in the NASA galaxy: the First National Bank put a space ship logo on its counter checks and developers dubbed the city's first shopping center the "Space Flight Plaza Mall." But Picayune's history, finally, has no single narrative backbone for a self-conscious history to cohere around until the late teens when the Crosbys arrived and both provided and forced such a backbone. But even that backbone was driven by economics and the dailiness of survival: even with all their generosity and interest in community the Crosbys supplied Picayune with continuity but not with a history.

Picayune's past is thus empty of the usual signifying and energizing gestures of history. It has no history that would define it as something other than itself, nothing, therefore, that would have allowed it to

---

*I am pleased to point to John Hawkins Napier III's *Lower Pearl River's Piney Woods: Its Land and People* (University, MS: The University of Mississippi Center for the Study of Southern Culture, 1985), from which I have shamelessly appropriated everything in this essay even remotely resembling a fact.

transcend itself as, say, Oxford has. Its history is flatly its own, and not peculiarly "southern" but merely the history of the whole United States.

iii.

Picayune's lack of a historical center is figured in its landscape. It is unlike Oxford, whose famous courthouse stands both *at* and *as* its center, is both its source and its focus. Oxford radiates politically and economically outward in a concentric appropriation of geography to its corporate self. Metaphorically and psychologically it gazes intently inward; its oldest buildings, on the Square, sit en face to each other and to the courthouse, so that to look outward is also to look inward. Their individual gazes constantly intersect and interact with each other and with the traffic: they are constantly alive to all four sides of people as they drive around the Square looking for parking places or walk, lingering here and there to jaw with friends on the public spaces of the courthouse lawn and the sidewalk.

Oxford's political and economic energy is thus equally based in reflection and action. Its history is an infinite baffle of resonances and myths and metaphors and fiction that may be, finally, fuller of signification than of event. There's a gracious plenty of event, God knows, but how much Oxford's events owe their designation as "event" to William Faulkner's signifying imagination we can only speculate; we may easily suppose that such an imagination might well have done for the lower Pearl River what Faulkner's did for north Mississippi. Precisely because that gargantuan imagination appropriated Oxford and turned it into a "literary" landscape, the town is so completely conscious of itself as a metaphor for other things that it may actually have become a metaphor for itself. But since the Square by which Oxford defines itself is also its own closed geographical landscape, the town does a good job of containing the metaphor and so not only resists entropy but actually makes of itself a dynamo that generates a very active life of engagement not just with its past but also with its present and its future.

Picayune, by contrast, has no such geographical or corporate center. It began more or less incidentally around the turn of the century as a freckling of sawmills and logging camps. The town itself was probably not even the locus of the camps and mills, but rather an eventual corporate and economic epicenter of sorts, its location occasioned by the advent of the railroad. Picayune's topography made it a logical spot for the New Orleans & Northeastern Railroad's switching yard. It lies just about at the point on the north-south axis where the land begins to rise significantly above the flattening sealevel land of the Gulf Coast regions: in the sixty miles from the coast to Picayune the terrain rises 70 feet; in the next six miles it rises to 170 feet above sea level. Long trains could cross the flatlands south with no trouble but could not climb the hillier lands north. Picayune became the point at which trains would split into two or three to go north and combine two or three into one to continue more economically on the return south. Folks built a depot, a hotel and café, and some other ramshackle businesses in an expanding cluster around the depot, right around the spot where Canal Street now crosses the tracks.

Picayune's main north-south thoroughfare seems to have been originally one leg of the old Jackson Military Road, one of several routes over which Andrew Jackson moved his army to Chalmette for the Battle of New Orleans. The route became U.S. Highway 11 in the mid-twenties; like the Military Road, Highway 11 intertwines with and plaits itself around the NO & NE (now the Southern) Railroad. Though the depot stayed put next the tracks until well into the sixties, when it was razed and not replaced, the other businesses seem to have moved about a half block east and re-established themselves loosely, shoulder to shoulder, up and down the eastern side of the highway: a hotel of course right across from the depot, eventually a postoffice next door and a bank, a drug store, hardware- and seed- and grocery- and general-stores, cafés and as the town grew inevitably others that catered not to needs but to desires: a dime store, a movie theatre, a jewelry store, eventually a bus station, and a fast-food outlet, Frostop, strung out up and down the highway, north and south, like independent beads on a rural string.

They all gazed in parallel lines westward. They could look all day and never see each other, indeed not see anything but profile: automobiles, trains, trucks, headed north or south; people too, unless they were coming in or leaving your store. People rarely parked and walked from one end of town to the other to do their shopping; they'd have to walk back, two ways in a straight line, not a trip around a square, not one direction but two or rather two instead of four, moving always athwart the westward gaze, and never with it or into it. And so the town's gaze was not communal or collective at all, but merely westward, as parallel with and separate from each other as were the railroad tracks that dictated the town's landscape, crossing the tracks and creating with them a sort of grid over the emptiness, and not even the illusion of confluence on the horizon, as tracks meet: no confluence of its individual gazes and so no collective vision. No center, no focus, for the collective gaze, no reflection: no conservation but a dissipation of its energies westward. But what west?

On a map the + formed by the intersection of Highway 11 and Canal Street would seem to be town center, but a map doesn't show how the railroad cuts a wide swath parallel to the highway, separating the east and west sides of town by a hundred yards of glinting steel ribs, unmowed weeds, and a space not particularly open, not even particularly desolate. It's not public or unclaimed or unappropriated space: it's just space, emptiness, thousands of squared yards of it, right through where city center should be. West Canal Street has to cross those tracks before it can meet up with its East Canal self at the highway. Except for two or three ramshackle buildings on the west side of the highway, between the tracks and the highway, partially blocking the westward view, this railroad space was mostly what the buildings on the east side had to look at: that, the trains in profile, heading north, heading south, obstructing traffic between East and West Picayune, and West Picayune itself, which, made up of businesses facing each other for two or three blocks along West Canal Street, didn't have to look back.

The two-storey Bank of Picayune building, on the northwest corner, dominates the intersection of Canal Street and Highway 11. On the southeast corner in the fifties was Bob's Jewelry, a neat awninged little green tile building, not so imposing as the bank, but part of a larger building, divided into several storefronts, that dominated the southern part of the highway. Both western corners are now empty; in the fifties there were service stations on both that sat several yards back from the intersection, surrounded by great open spaces of curbless concrete, spaces differentiated from Canal Street and the highway only by the smoothness of the concrete. The service stations sat back from the highway, as though in retreat from the traffic, which might suck them along in its wake, and perhaps from the more imposing structures across the street. Bob's Jewelry and the buildings southeast of the intersection sit as close to the streets, the traffic, as the sidewalks will let them, and their awnings seem to reach into the street itself. The bank sits alone on the northeast corner, its parking lot to its immediate north separating it from Picayune Drug. The bank also sits aggressively close to the intersection; its main entrance opens catercorner directly into it, facing the traffic light in its center, as if standing sentinel against any that might either run the light or steal it.

East Picayune's north-south halves are mostly symmetrical with each other, built as they are upon streets and avenues that intersect and interlock at right angles, moving eastward from and parallel to

Highway 11. West Picayune, on the other hand, looks a little bit like a fan opened out, a Y whose arms move toward the northwest and the southwest, uncompacting itself as it ambles toward the Pearl River, though obviously what the angles actually reflect is the town's general constitutive movement from the Pearl to the railroad center of town.

The City Hall, built in the late thirties, sits in a tiny needle-angled lot where Goodyear Boulevard and Williams Avenue intersect. One block behind it is the First Baptist Church and, further west on the Boulevard, sit the high school, the hospital, the Catholic Church, and a huge structure that Picayune built to try to lure some sort of manufacturing industry into the town, with only middling success over the years. Further west a fairly substantial series of nice residences line the boulevard. At the end of the boulevard, where it tees into Beech Street, sits Crosby Chemicals, the retort, where during my boyhood tung nuts were turned into paint, turpentine, and other home supply necessities that helped drive Picayune's economy.

The City Hall is a tallish—three stories—red brick building, modern and modest by courthouse standards, with building-wide gray concrete steps leading up to the front entrance, which was for years the entrance to the public library. In the fifties the building contained all you'd expect of municipal offices: the mayor's and city manager's offices and all the city tax-assessing and record-keeping, the courtroom, the fire department, the police department, the jail, and the public library. It sits across Williams Avenue from, but not facing, the building that housed McDonald Funeral Home, catercornered to but not facing the building that housed Crosby Dairy Products; it faced, but only at its 20-degree angle, the parking lot and the blank north wall of the Jitney Jungle grocery store on Main Street; its back is turned to the First Baptist Church, which itself sits facing the boulevard rather than City Hall; there may be a couple of homes across the boulevard which face it directly, but City Hall looks at nothing but its own diminishing front yard. Unlike its Oxford counterpart, it looks at nothing and avoids, in turn, being looked at.

i v .

One of the things that provided Picayune with some continuity, perhaps even saved its life, was the advent of the Crosby family, a burly group of lumbermen from Crosby, in the Southwest part of Mississippi, south of Natchez. Attracted to the rich possibilities of Piney Woods timber, they arrived in the area in the late teens; unlike others in the timber industry who came, cut, and got out, the Crosbys from the start made a long-term commitment to the area, to its people and its natural resources. They came, or at least they stayed, not in the traditional spirit of southern self-aggrandizement, like Thomas Sutpen or the Little Foxes, but in a quite unconventional and forward-looking spirit of understanding that to a large degree their own welfare was intimately tied to the welfare of the larger community.

The Crosbys I knew were the family of L. O. Jr., father of Lynn, several years older than I, and of Osmond III, my age and a very good friend through our years in Picayune. Dorothy, their wife and mother, was a transplanted North Dakotan who brought to Picayune and to me a variety of outworld sophistications: there was in the Crosby mansion a personal and well-used library off the master bedroom and opera—*opera!*—in the record cabinet downstairs.

L. O.'s commitment to the area stemmed from an actual love of the forest, a commitment to both its commercial uses and its preservation. He knew the woods, a lot of which he owned, not just as commercial property but as something huge and friendly that needed nurturing and caring for. He was an avid outdoorsman, a hunter and a fisherman, a magnanimous supporter of the Boy Scouts, which organization honored him with its highest award, the Silver Buffalo. He was instrumental in the construction of Camp Ti'ak, a Boy Scout camp near Wiggins, Mississippi, and supported it both financially and personally; he would occasionally accompany Oz and the rest of us to the camp, or visit us there, and would go on hikes with us through the woods, supplementing our handbook readings about woodcraft with his own observations, taking obvious pleasure in pointing out the differences between fabulous varieties of trees and other woodland vegetation. He was also an author, the first person I ever knew to have actually written a book, *Cecil in the Yukon*, about a hunting trip to Alaska he and a group of friends had taken. He was the richest person in Picayune and, so far as I knew from my own experience, one of the sweetest-tempered and most reasonable and least presumptuous people I have ever known.

I don't want to sentimentalize L. O., or depict him as softhearted or -headed. Clearly he was not. No one who accomplished what he did could have been addled: over the years he and his family built a huge lumbering business and several related industries in the area, ranging from the lumber mill itself to Crosby Dairy Products, to Crosby Chemicals, a laboratory that made and marketed paint, turpentine, and other by-products of pine trees, and then of tung trees, which the Crosbys imported into south Mississippi from Japan in order to manufacture paint and varnish from the juice of the tung nut. The Crosbys employed hundreds of people, probably thousands, over the years.

For my purposes, L. O. is equally important for what he was not as for what he was. Given his enormous economic influence in the area, he was in a position to become the town patriarch, one of the Big Daddys or Will Varners fabled in southern myth and literature, one who controls the town's economy by owning the mill or the plantation and so holding its people in a kind of peonage in which all tribute runs upward to the fount. I suspect that there are those who believe that he was such a patriarch, but in fact he wasn't.

His father was a founder of the Goodyear Yellow Pine Company, which was established in Picayune in 1916 and became a parent company of many related wood product industries. He first became involved in the family's business during the Great Depression, managing a rehabilitation effort to ease conditions of the unemployed associated with the lumber industry in the Picayune area. He developed experimental crops such as satsumas, peaches, strawberries, and tung trees on cutover land, and began a program of truck farming. At the beginning of World War II he took charge of his father's company, diversifying its holdings and rebuilding the business. He later became the president and general manager of Crosby Forest Products of Picayune (formerly Goodyear Yellow Pine Company). He was responsible for the construction in Picayune of plants making wirebound boxes, treating wood, and extracting tung oil; he was continually responding, for the good of the community—and of the Crosbys—to the demands and the opportunities provided by local, national, and even international economies.

He constantly re-invested himself and his money in the community from which he had gained so much. During the Depression, for example, when there was no market for the lumber and when his employees were out of work, he supplied employees with tools and with seed, at no cost to them, and so gave them the means at least to feed themselves when they had no money. He ran for and was twice elected mayor, subjecting himself to the general approbation. He was among the biggest supporters of the Picayune High School band's trips to march in the 1956 Rose Bowl parade in Pasadena, California, and the 1959 Macy's Thanksgiving Day Parade in New York City, spending lots of his own money to feed all 150 of us and to ensure that we were able to make the most of the opportunities that this kind of travel had given us. He invested heavily in Picayune's physical, cultural, and religious health, donating money for the construction of the L. O. Crosby Sr. Memorial Hospital, for the Margaret Reed Crosby Library, and for a memorial chapel at the First

Baptist Church. These are just the public offerings; I have no doubt that he aided and abetted other enterprises in ways not so public. In short, his was an entrepreneurial spirit quite at odds with the acquisitive, Snopesish, local baron of popular southern myth and literature, who ruthlessly exploits and rules with an iron fist all within his demesne, a sort of southern "Godfather." L. O. was by no means that.

Without the Crosbys, without their efforts to stabilize the economy in hard times, Picayune might easily have gone the way of Pearlington and Gainesville: it might have disappeared as a factor in the region's economy, its people dispersed to other places looking for work, and so replaying the pattern of transience that makes Picayune less a "place" in any traditional southern sense than a brief conjunction of time and space where people stop, momentarily, in their efforts to get somewhere else.

v.

Picayune has a history, of course, but it has no single *story*, no single narrative thread, not even narrative contrarieties, that provide a locus for all its chronologies to cohere around. It's an apt illustration of Faulkner's description in *Requiem for a Nun* of historical *event* as "litter from the celestial experimental workbench." Folks moving forward in time, ferociously or even timidly confronting the pure possibility of the future, have only minimal time for pattern; plan as we will, exert what control we can, the future still comes at us as a chaos of the possible, a daunting variety of pressures and forces, of causes and effects, of coincidences, of accidents. It gets carved into a shape as we choose which of the contending pressures to deal with, how to deal with them: whether to confront them head on or to deflect into the path of least resistance, whether to hide in the sand. In any case, we shape our lives looking forward, grabbling at what we need for the moment, discarding what we don't need, choosing among the options and clinging to what seems likely to make things better. Folks looking at the future need only patterns of predictability to do the kinds of planning and goal-setting that are essential to any productive life; but we quickly abandon or revise these predictions when we confront new opportunities that we can take advantage of. The future holds nothing inevitable or necessary or fixed: it cannot, or it is dead.

We shape our lives forward, but we write our histories backward, of course, to explain—to justify or excuse—the present. Victors looking backward write histories that depict their victories not as a victories of a more powerful force over a less powerful one but rather as the necessary victory of right over wrong (all victories are victories of ideology)—without saying, and perhaps not even realizing, that victors get to define "right" and "wrong" *because* they won. Southern history's edge comes from the fact that it is often written by the losers, the victims—or in any case the apologists, the mythmongers—whose moral position is that something went wrong: what was it? Southerners cannot admit that the South was wrong, because *being right* is so intimately central to everything in the southerner's life, from fundamentalist religion to conservative politics. Being right, more than anything else, animates the notion of southern "honor." But if we were *right*, how could we have been beaten?

Thus southern apologists and other fiction writers often construct a history that is primarily concerned to find ways for us to be, to have been, right in spite of losing, and this is why, I think, southerners are so passionate about history. We cannot talk of victories, so we talk of courage, of manners, of gentility, of paternalism, of the bastardly conduct of the Yankees, of *their* perfidy, their general soullessness.

We massage ourselves with the idea that we are not agoraphobic or racist, and take sophistical pride in arguments that the Civil War was not about slavery but rather about economics; that our problems are not our fault but the fault of circumstances we had no control over; that we are a fine and genteel, a morally superior people, whose way of life was destroyed by infidels who keep us under siege. We memorialize Jefferson Davis's home in Biloxi and the planters who built the beautiful antebellum homes in Natchez and Columbus and Holly Springs, and we do so without one single word about the slaves upon whose backs those houses, those white lives, were built. Incredibly, we regularly reenact battles *that we lost*—not, as more than one wag has suggested, in the hope that we'll eventually get it right, but simply as an agon, a passion, a pageantry of our martyrdom.

Thus we romanticize and spiritualize defeat; we tell stories of the doomed charge against overwhelming odds, of our brave boys dying in and for a Cause lost from the beginning not because we were wrong but because we were finally outnumbered by the soulless Yankees. We stress the tales of gallantry, of heroism, of courage and character; of ex-slaves who loved ol' Miss and ol' Massa so much they stayed around, even helping to fight the Yankees; of women at home sewing the flags, being beautiful and faithful, tending the wounded.

We are still tending the wounded, still constructing a past that will let us be both right and defeated, that will permit us to transcend our shabby and problematic present, which falls far short of what a righteous people deserve. Failing to transcend ourselves, we force transcendence on to immanent reality, to try to control the present and the future in the terms of our moral positions, so that things don't get any worse. Our fundamentalism is thus very much of a piece with our politics, since our politics, like our religion, is heavily fraught with the moral problematics of right and wrong not as factors in negotiating behavior through a complex and complicated world, but as absolutes handed down from a Controlling Hand that presides not just over the past but over the future too—or would, of course, if not for the pernicious forces challenging the moral order.

Southern myths often seem to exist independently of the South itself, or at least independently of such as Picayune—places which, I suspect, are legion. After all, there are only a finite number of minié balls and Civil War battles, and an infinite number of such towns as Picayune. But southern history is almost completely defined by the narratives of the Shilohs, the Vicksburgs, the Oxfords, Birminghams, Selmas, Philadelphias, and Jacksons, where life-and-death dramas gave the historical landscape some vivid, clarifying images to cohere around, like Wallace Stevens's jar in Tennessee (probably, in Tennessee, a Mason jar); whether combatants littered the grounds with bodies or merely shot bulletholes in the courthouse columns, these were the sites where good and evil demonstrably slugged it out and where southerners lost everything but the spirit to keep fighting. Southern culture gets defined downward from that spirit, in terms of the people who cling to the verities of the past in order to avoid the complications of the present and the looming predicted disaster that the future holds.

Americans sentimentalize history; southerners are perhaps the worst of all, though clearly Bostonians revere Paul's famous ride in much the same way that a Charlestonian gets moony about Fort Sumter. This is really curious to me, because in fact Americans don't have very much history. As republics go, we are very young indeed, still perhaps retain a good deal of the high spirits of the early settlers, who thought of North America as a place to start history over, and we write history, especially southern history, to deal with our mystification over our derailment from those high ideals and expectations, those grand false heroic hopes. Where did we go wrong?

Southern history gets defined, legitimately, as a resistance to change, and the sites of that resistance—Oxford, Selma, Bull Run, Shiloh—get deified by the forces that cling to quasi-religious ideas that once there was a golden age where all values—and people—were in their proper places. Southerners, the Fugitives and the Agrarians and their progeny especially, deify nature, the rural, as being very near to Edenic splendor and therefore closer to what Faulkner called the "old eternal verities," which by their eternal nature are unchanging but which in a commercial, historical world are constantly under attack by unrighteous forces of change (the North) and so need constant defending. We have thus learned from that cultural oligarchy operating out of Nashville, from other critics, and from fictional characters like Faulkner's Isaac McCaslin, to sentimentalize the southern wilderness far beyond the range of the most intense of tree-hugging environmentalists: a tree falls or a bear gets killed or somebody moves into the city and we get loopy thinking about how terrible change is.

Change, for southerners like Isaac McCaslin, equals loss, deprivation, separation. For many authors too, though not, I'd argue, for Faulkner and Eudora Welty. Faulkner recognized the problematics of change but roared at us the necessity to cope with change always, because the refusal to change, to be part of history, is to become static and die, and readers who take McCaslin's sentimentalization of the past as Faulkner's miss Faulkner's radical critique of that way of viewing the past, in *Go Down, Moses* and other works. Eudora Welty goes one step further; for her, change is not intimidating. For many of her characters, value lies not at all in the old verities but in new ones waiting to be discovered by folks with the courage to face the new configurations of political and social order that new values—change—might bring about. We need to embrace the future, see it not as daunting and fearful but as freedom, possibility.

v i .

Picayune, my home town, seems to have gotten along perfectly well without a tragic sense of history and without mustering its collective courage to face a problematic future. Picayune gets along fine without a theme and without a moral. It is neither static, backward-looking, nor overly invested in or concerned with futures, though it certainly has tried to take advantage of opportunity when, through no fault nor action of its own, opportunity knocked. It worships its ancestors only to the extent of a monument to the dead of World Wars I and II, dedicated in 1989, and though it tried to wrap itself around and ride NASA into the future, NASA didn't, finally, give it the economic jump-start it had hoped for; but no matter. Picayune didn't define an era, but it did considerably more than just muddle through: it's less than a staging place for history but considerably more than a bump in the historical road. It bubbled up out of the south Mississippi wilderness as a response more to a circumstance than to a real need; it was one of several sites that could have provided what it provided to the area. Picayune didn't define anything; it doesn't represent or stand for anything but itself.

But that's no matter either. That is in fact enough, for the thousands of folks who filtered through there, who came and stayed for a day, a year, a lifetime, passing through on the way to somewhere else. The only thing "grotesque" about Picayune, southern though it be, is its allconsuming American *normalcy*; but that, of course, can be grotesque and terrifying enough.

My Father, Flem Snopes

I Sonned a Father

I sonned a father who would not be sonned, broke
My child's heart to show him blood that bade me
Insecurely sit where he could see
My courage running out toward his, accused
By keen investing eyes that could not bear
To see me err or give me grace to think
That I could be forgiven my uselessness.
I watched him grow, nurtured him patiently with
My need, accepted all he returned of love
Or judgment, and watched him die within a minute
Of the day he could have looked at me in peace,
Or not have looked at all.
                              Unsonned fathers
Make their sons survive them: the final blow.

I did not know my father at a time when he was becoming; he seemed always to be the unchanging same, the force I had to deal with until long after he died one summer evening in my twenty-sixth year, massively and unforgivably died, while I was becoming the fluid, negotiating self I was to be for the next thirty years. He died without absolving me of taking up space in his life and, more, without teaching me that only I could absolve myself of that. I have done so, and now in my turn am trying, in middleaged retrograde, to absolve him of the space he continues to take up in mine, space I could put to better use.

I have now outlived him by two years, yet I see him more and more often in the mirrors I look into, in the squat genetic shaping of my body to his. Getting to and passing the age at which he died was more of a hurdle than I thought it would be; I faced that moment, and the ones subsequent, with increasing fears that I am more mortally than empathetically his son. I can claim only an amateur psychologist's understanding of him, and that mostly by analogy with my own middleaging and my own experiences as husband and father. I have no idea what he felt or thought, whether he thought at all, whether he thought he had time for or needed reflection.

For years I was convinced of the wisdom of his every motive, the judiciousness of his every decision, which were instantaneous and infallible and therefore terrifying. He seemed to have an unerring sense of what he wanted and how to get it—a design, if you will, to which those motives and decisions were subordinate and which made them inevitable. I don't know how much of what he wanted he actually got, but I suspect not all of it. He probably didn't know precisely what he wanted, but he knew he was more likely to find it in town than in the country, somewhere other than home. He mostly wanted to escape the farm that he hated, to escape whatever of hardship or ignominy he connected with poverty and rural life. More than anything he wanted respect and respectability, two different but not incompatible things.

He left little to analyze except memory, which is always clouded over with desire and regret. He left few written documents, no monuments other than at the cemetery, no mansions to decay or to be preserved on the historical register, no legends enshrining courage or ruthlessness, no abortive dynasties to purge him or to grovel in his memory, no burdensome enigmas for his descendants to worry over or be ashamed about or live down. Still, he accomplished a good deal more than survival.

He was plenty ambitious; if hard work or desire were the arbiters of success he would have been rolling in it. He might have been Faulkner's

Thomas Sutpen had his times and topography been more amenable to his ambitions. Perhaps for this reason my most earthshaking insight into Faulkner (it may have been only I who shook) was the discovery of how much alike he and Faulkner's Flem Snopes were. I didn't have any real sense of either until I understood them both, in an epiphanic flash one scholarly evening. To understand this, however, requires a bit more sympathy with Flem Snopes than we have been accustomed to have.

Like Flem, my father largely succeeded where Thomas Sutpen did not because Sutpen wanted to subdue his culture, to overwhelm it, to be better, grander, stronger than it was, so that he would not be vulnerable to it. But he didn't choose to battle it on its own turf and terms; instead he betook himself to a frontier outpost in north Mississippi where the competition wasn't nearly so stiff and where he could more completely control the terms of his engagement with that culture which had both spawned and spurned him. He thought he could create his own version of that culture and create himself at the same time, create a life and a world outside of history, its and his own; he thought that by being bigger and grander he could stand in overpowering opposition to that existing world. But as *Absalom, Absalom!* tells us, history indeed catches up with him and he can't elude the terms of engagement that the existing culture always dictates, even that ragged parcel of it in isolated north Mississippi. Flem and my father, however, moved as quickly as they could into an urban world—Flem into Jefferson, my father into Picayune, the very seats of the culture they wanted in to—and they succeeded where Sutpen failed through a more problematic, perhaps more insidious tactic: they mastered their culture not by subduing it but by yielding completely to it, by absorbing it, *becoming* it. In this, Flem Snopes beat my father hands down. But my father was well on his way when he died.

Flem succeeds by making of himself a mirror in which the Jefferson and Frenchman's Bend folks can see an ideal form of themselves—what they want to be; he does this incidentally, in pursuit not so much of a dream, like Sutpen, but of an image. In his early days he doesn't know the difference between dream and image and his late discovery of that difference is his undoing. He becomes, indeed, the "model citizen." Those who lack our readers' knowledge of his history (as opposed to his origins) are likely to see Flem primarily as a savvy trader, a hardworking (and even suspiciously honest) salesman, the husband (even if a cuckold) of a beautiful wife, the vice president and then the president of the bank, the grieving widower of a suicide, a Baptist deacon. Sutpen wants folks to look at him and marvel; he wants the power to open and close the doors upon the outside world. Flem, by contrast, wins, if win he does, by becoming a modernist Gorgon; more, he is not only the Gorgon but also the very mirror-shield that the cultural Perseus would fight him with. Thus in the battle with Flem, Perseus—in the Snopes Trilogy it is Gavin Stevens—turns himself to stone because in his mirror-shield he can see only himself, a sight more terrifying than the original Gorgon, more petrifying because, looking at himself, Perseus cannot see the horror he has set himself to destroy. Horror always looks like somebody else. In Faulkner, respectability, mindless cultural conformity, is that very mirror. Flem's prime insidiousness lies in the fact that his victory is a victory for bourgeois culture. Sutpen tries to suck the culture dry; Flem colludes with it in mutual nourishment. Flem and his culture reify each other and Flem becomes, in *The Mansion*, the very "pillar, rock-fixed, of things as they are." It remains to be seen whether Flem or Sutpen is the greater victim: Sutpen at least achieves some tragic grandeur; Flem fades into the walls of respectability, goes down not even swinging but just empty.

Thus Flem does not hide his vices, which he and the culture, of course, think are virtues. Flem's great power, his leg up on everybody else, is that he profoundly understands the human longing to possess the signs that certify and affirm a person's place in the culture; he understands this better than any character in Faulkner save his wife, Eula Varner, and the old marshal in *A Fable*, to whom Flem and Sutpen are intimately related. People's passionate engagement with their dreams, their illusions, render them vulnerable and so give Flem power over them. *Sanctuary's* Popeye caters to people's vices, Flem to their dreams; Faulkner and Flem know that people are much more vulnerable to their dreams than to their vices.

Faulkner doesn't tell us enough about Flem's ratiocinative processes or his feelings for us to know how completely he understands the passion of the American Dream itself or to know the level at which he responds personally to it. It is hard to think of Flem as having feelings deep enough to be called a passion or a dream; but he is clearly aware of the uses to which passion and dreams can be put, and his analytical side must be constantly amazed at how eagerly people will bare their backsides or throw their egg money at him for some piece of their dreams, however diminished and unsatisfactory a piece they may have to settle for— spotted horses indeed! For Flem, any single element of the dream (Eula or the Old Frenchman place, for example) is merely another stepping stone or a negotiating chip or a building block to be used in constructing the total edifice of his design.

Unillusioned himself—not *dis*illusioned, just *un*—, Flem has al- most unrestricted access to the illusions of others, a most powerful position. Faulkner recounts Flem's life in the Snopes Trilogy as a sort of testing or trying out of the various forms that the American Dream takes. Flem hopes, one assumes, to master the forms and then to discover the content in the forms; but he finds at the last that for all its size and scope, his own columned mansion, that preeminent sign of his and Faulkner's culture, is empty of meaning and gives way to the primitive destructive passion of cousin Mink. More's the pity, he does not have the capacity to discover that his mansion is empty because he is empty. Flem's life proves, finally, how completely the myths of the American Dream seduce folks into the hedonistic paradox. Through Flem, then, Faulkner suggests that only by not believing in the American Dream can you hope to possess it; otherwise, like the culture, it possesses you, sucks you dry and goes its own way, nourished by your substance, leaving you empty.

i i.

Like Flem, my father wanted to escape his origins: not a bad desire, of itself, and easier to understand if you don't—like a lot of city folks, like a lot of urban and otherwise urbane critics who have swallowed the Fugitives' agrarian line—sentimentalize rural life. It is quite simple to understand, however, if you can see things from the point of view of the escapee, the real twentieth-century fugitive, who makes those ideologues from Nashville look like Bossman on a chain gang. I've no doubt that some real sense of the possibilities of the American Dream drove my father almost from the beginning; I've also no doubt that he was less driven by the dream than by the white-hot burning desire not to have to spend the rest of his life plowing to make a living. All of the children, he and all his siblings except his older sister Virgie, moved away from the country as soon as they could. He never talked much about farming, and so I cannot identify from the highway any crop less obvious than corn or cotton in bloom.

He turned his back to, if not on, his rural origins and, like Scarlett O'Hara, swore never to be poor again. He moved to Picayune in 1939. He was twenty-two, with a high school education, a fugitive from the Depression in rural Mississippi (where, he told me, the Depression didn't have much impact: hardly anybody could tell the difference). Picayune was incidental; his father came to pastor at a church in Nicholson, a couple of miles south, and he followed to seek his fortune in the big city. He took a job as a night clerk in a service station owned by Bill Alexander, spent his days moonlighting by borrowing one of Alexander's pickup trucks and driving satsumas to Monticello to sell, so that he could visit my mother-to-be.

When he and Mother got married Alexander raised his salary from $15 to $20 a week. They moved to Picayune and had a son who lived not quite a year; recovered, and got me in early 1943; he was inducted into the army and was wounded in Italy; after the war he returned to get my brother in 1947. He worked as a chief clerk for Schrock's Western Auto Associate Store and then for a while for Bo Stevens in a similar capacity. From them he learned the trade. In 1953 he decided he wanted to be the boss himself; he bought a Firestone Tire & Rubber Company franchise, and sold Firestone tires and Philco appliances for the rest of his life.

He was hard-working, driven even; he was tense, very tightly wound, and I learned very quickly not to come up behind him, not to surprise him, and especially not to touch him from behind, since he always reacted from some selfprotecting impulse. I once watched Sedgie Fillingame come in the store and, to get his attention, touch him on the shoulder. He was doing something with a pencil in his hand; he whirled around suddenly, sharply, to his right, his right arm extended to ward off the attack. The pencil point ripped a big hole in Sedgie's shirtfront; his fist took a button with it as it passed through. It was as quick a reaction as anything I had ever seen, completely reflexive; another quarter of an inch and he would have hurt Sedgie seriously. Sedgie turned pale, my father no less so, and after the initial moment, then the several moments of discomfiture, apology, and reassurance had passed, Sedgie asked his question, got his answer, and walked quietly away.

My father explained his nerves as the result of his experiences in Italy. No doubt: I have seen him tremble watching news footage of the Korean War on television; he would not, did not at any rate, talk very much about the war, and would not watch a movie in which there were battle scenes. I suspect that he suffered from a version of what we now call post-trauma stress syndrome most of his life, and that that was at the base of a lot of his, and our, problems. My mother and my Aunt Virginia assure me that he returned from the War a different person. But I, of course, didn't know him before the War and so had nothing to compare him to, no reason to compare him to anything but my own need.

Few documents survive from his life: some artifacts—a Purple Heart, a scattering of photographs, his voice on an old reel-to-reel tape that he made at the store (I no longer own a machine I can play it on), a hand-written copy of a devotional he gave in his Sunday school, a few letters and postcards he wrote to Mother and me from Italy, as though he were there as a tourist. I have one of the Firestone store's account books, the ledgers on which he kept up with what people owed him; that's the last I'll write of ledgers and accounts payable. The writer in me wants to make that ledger into a metaphor, but the critic won't permit something that obvious; perhaps the debtor in me can't deal with it. The Purple Heart reminds me that he was nearly killed in World War II, hit by shrapnel from an exploding grenade, though the wound was deeper than a mere grenade can reach. Mother has kept the telegram the government sent notifying her that he had been wounded but was otherwise all right and headed back into duty. How often and with what irony have I read that message.

He was a genuine country boy from southwestern Mississippi. His family were Depression-poor, but whether they were what other folks, then or now, would have called white trash I don't know, though I don't believe so. His father was a Southern Baptist preacher—if not an actual itinerant then one who moved around so much that I've never been able to get a fix on where he pastored the longest. Several older people now tell me that they remember him as a pastor. He was a tall, kindly looking man. I remember seeing him preach but do not remember anything he said; he died at the age of fifty-seven, when I was four.

My father was never very specific about life at home, or at least I don't remember that he said much beyond a few stories about how he hated plowing and, with some glee, how much his father had enjoyed whipping his children—and how much he did too: one of the reasons you have kids, he said. I knew when he said this that he was mostly kidding, but there was a considerable degree of truth in it too. He thought swift and judicious punishment a duty, not a pleasure, though who ever to know how much of pleasure obtains in the duties of power? I don't know how hard or how often his father whipped him. I know how often and how hard mine whipped me, with a belt, on a bare butt and, terrifying and painful as that was, I remember only too well how much less terrifying and painful the whippings were than his disapproval was; what became my own relentless and now residual expectation of that disapproval was worse than anything and the whippings themselves were at times an actual relief. I can't say how much he enjoyed it, only how often he practiced it, and I can only speculate from what we now know about how such relationships repeat themselves from generation to generation that he stood in much the same relation to his father as I to him, though to be sure my Aunt Virginia tells me that she remembers my grandmother, not my grandfather, as the family's disciplinarian.

In 1953 he opened Polk's Firestone Dealer Store—the "Dealer" stuck so clumsily in there to let all of Picayune know that Polk's Firestone, unlike Hal Schrock's Western Auto *Associate* Store, was locally owned and operated and should be patronized in order to keep our money circulating at home. The store's essential product was tires but we also sold various other appliances and devices for home and auto: refrigerators, ranges, washers and dryers, lawn mowers and parts, shotguns and rifles, fishing gear, radios and televisions and hi-fi equipment. It was a small hardware version of an old-fashioned general store and a risky proposition, since there were at least three or four other similar stores in small-city Picayune, stores much larger and better equipped, much older and more established in the community, with a wider range of choices.

I was ten in 1953. I spent my teen years watching and, I like to think, helping him build a business. He kept citing frightening statistics about the number of failures among newly-started businesses like his and vowing that that was not going to happen to him—us. I never did know, still don't know, how he managed to make a decent living; perhaps I don't want to know. I don't know what combination of the power of his personality, the quality of the Firestone and Philco line of products, dogged hard work, under-the-table financial deals, or simple good luck made the Firestone store a go. He did work hard. He left home early, sometimes way before dawn, and came home late, sometimes spending twenty or so hours a day at one or another aspects of the business. He could afford to employ only two or three people at any given time—a bookkeeper, a salesman/assistant manager, someone to change the tires, to deliver and install air conditioners and washing machines—so he had to tend to a lot of the store's activities himself, both managerial and menial: delivering appliances, changing tires, repairing lawn mower engines, installing TV antennas. When bookkeeperless, he would sometimes go the store at four A.M. to post the previous day's receipts, before opening the doors at seven. When he closed at six P.M., he would come home for supper, then perhaps head back to the store to catch up on the lawn mower engines that had been brought in for repair; frequently he would then go "collecting," looking for people who were behind in their payments, tracking them down in their homes and if necessary repossessing the item they had bought. Sometimes I would go with him, when the item to be repossessed was so large he couldn't handle it by himself; but he could singlehandedly load almost anything into the pickup, even a large refrigerator. I could too, after some practice.

By 1968 he had indeed made a go of the store; it was beginning to pay off in all the ways he wanted it to. As he became successful, he was invited to join the Rotary Club, and was very proud to associate with some of Picayune's older and more distinguished people. He became a deacon in the First Baptist Church. He became a Shriner. He and Mother hung out with Dr. and Mrs. Kety, two prominent citizens, and often took off with them for an evening in New Orleans to dine. He bought nice clothes in Dallas when we went there to visit his brother Austin, and he enjoyed telling about the shopping, the purchase. Picayune wasn't big enough for him.

For fifteen years he worked like a dog, as we southerners say, to make a go of it, and died of a heart attack, his first, on a hot July day in 1968, literally from the strain of overwork, changing a huge truck tire (a very complicated and physically demanding process in those days), because there was nobody else to do it.

I fear that much in this minimalist sketch of his life will leave the impression that I accuse him of Babbitry, of a shallow chamber-of-commerce quest for material certification; that I present him as a parody of the American Dream. Nothing could be further from the truth. Indeed, that is precisely the opposite impression I want to create. There is nothing parodic about his life, certainly not if seen from his own point of view or that of his family or even of thousands of others across the South who shared that same quest. You can see the outlines of parody only if you are sufficiently a Have as to see him and his like as pretenders. He wasn't pretending. Not a bone in his body was faking anything. He desperately wanted a share of the good life and it wasn't his fault if he didn't have the luxuries of place and fortune that would have allowed him some, any, distance on himself and his dream—luxuries that I do have, largely thanks to him. He was too seriously involved in escape and survival to see himself, or to allow anyone else to see him, as anything to laugh about. It is essential to grant him the absolute dignity and seriousness of purpose that he invested his own life with.

He hated life in the country, but life in the city was also a serious, serious business. He told me that he often had to do things to survive in business that were unethical, though he was never very specific about what those things were. I have often wondered why he told me about these activities—to keep me from discovering them independently, perhaps, though I did so little with the store's financial records that that was not really likely. To implicate me? I doubt it, since he knew I had no plans to inherit the store and its good will. To be honest with me about the real world? To confess?

The city presented more serious problems, too. I ran across a picture of him during his early days in Picayune some years ago when I was reading through microfilm copies of the Picayune *Item*. The accompanying story reported that he had been the victim of a holdup at Bill Alexander's service station, on the main drag of town, where Canal Street crosses Highway 11. The thieves held a gun to his head, forced him to the floor, and fled with the cash in the till and a full tank of gas. He never mentioned it and I didn't discover it until long after he was dead. I doubt that he forgot it, as I cannot.

I have tried to meditate on this scene, without much luck. I would like to structure my way into his mind as he lay on that cold floor waiting for those invasive strangers to empty the cash register and perhaps to shoot his young life casually through the head, but I cannot do it, boggling perhaps at the picture of my own life spread so receptively there upon a cold grease-stained gas station floor, my own preemption a cold barrel nuzzling behind my notyet father's ear. Perhaps it's just that I cannot impute fear or helplessness to him, not even at twenty-two. Try as I might, I cannot impose on him at twenty-two what I would have felt at twenty-two or any other age with a gun at my head (though of course that gun *was* at my head). He must have felt fear and helplessness, as he must have felt them later, during the War; this perhaps explains why he would not speak of either or at least did not, since to speak of them would admit not weakness but vulnerability—which, like respect and respectability, are different but not incompatible. What is respectability anyway but a shoring up against vulnerability?

What really terrified him in the city, I suspect, was of another order altogether. The summer following my tenth grade, I think it was, he and I worked the Firestone Store mostly by ourselves: just the two of us to do all the store's activities of selling, sweeping, installing, delivering, collecting. In some ways we were closer than ever, but the summer was unrelenting in its pressure on both of us, he to make a living, I to get along with him, to contribute. I worked most days from 7 A.M. to 6 P.M. or so; it was one of those several stretches when he started at 3 or 4 A.M. and didn't come home until around midnight, sometimes later. If I sometimes went home at lunch (which we called dinner), he frequently didn't, and I'd bring him a plate lunch or a sandwich; Mother would even more frequently bring us both a meal of some sort. Usually around closing time he would tell me to bring the display merchandise—lawn mowers and cane fishing poles—in from the front, to drive the pickup home and he'd call me or Mother when he was ready to leave. We locked the rear entrance to the store from the inside, so that when we went home together in the evening, one of us would go out the back and drive the pickup to the front while the other locked the back door and met the truck at the front.

On this evening he told me to go ahead home and he'd call. We lived barely a half mile from the store and, because I wanted to walk and dawdle and probably because I just didn't want to be obligated to come back to get him later, I brought the truck around, parked it in front where he'd have to see it, then began my mindless walk home. I had not gone five blocks when he caught up with me. He jerked the truck over toward the sidewalk I was on, slammed the brakes, and said "Get in this truck, boy." He was angrier than I had ever seen him. He spoke softly, but I could hear him over the blaring retributive squeal of the brakes. I got in, shaken, not knowing what I had done; but this was a more or less permanent condition, not knowing what I had done that would eventually turn out to be wrong: waiting for the axe to fall. He jerked the truck into first gear, pulled off so hard my head bumped against the back window, and sped the rest of the way home as if running from something. He turned into our driveway, lurched to a gravelly stop behind our new high-finned Chrysler and said, "I don't work twenty hours a day to pay for a car and a truck so that my family has to be seen *walking*," and he leaned over me and opened the door. I couldn't even think, much less say, "But I wanted to walk. I *wanted* to." I could only get out of the truck, watch him slam into reverse, slew backwards out into the street, and gun it on back in the direction of the store.

I am still stunned by this, forty years later; even then I knew that it came from out of nowhere, both its intensity and its devastating originality. It was light years outside the widest range of errors I thought I might ever be guilty of: walking home. From this distance I can attribute motives, probable causes, and I have tried to teach myself that to understand is to forgive: who to know what encounter with what richer folks at the Rotary Club, what innocent jest, what crack, overheard by what improbable chance, had set him off, reminded him of his many long walks to town or to a neighbors' or even just of the time when he didn't have other transportation than his feet? Even so, I cannot account for, or forgive, his exceptional fury over my walking home. Understanding and forgiveness are not the same, not necessarily even related.

I do not remember what passed for the next three or four hours, whether I talked to Mother about what had happened or not, whether I actually cried or, as usual, just bore it silently, loud as it was. I only see myself in my bed in my room at the front of the house, in the dark, wide awake and wishing I—or he—were dead, wishing I could figure out how to make him happy somehow, not suspecting that he was probably even unhappier than I and less likely than I ever to understand what he'd done. I lay there opening myself to hatred, almost convincing myself of its power to immobilize him, to shut him out of my emotional concerns: it was the only power I had over him. And then came the only apology he ever offered me, an apology which, in being even more complicated than the affront, denied me that saving hatred.

Lying there, in more than one kind of darkness, I had no idea of the time. I heard the house's reverberating wood signal his arrival home. He and Mother talked, I do not know about what; perhaps she remonstrated with him. Some time later, long enough for him to have stewed, bathed, prepared for bed, he came to my room. I was preternaturally aware of every sound as he walked the long hall toward my room. He knocked and I said "come in." He opened the door in the dark and I remembered in a flash that I hadn't closed the door to the cedar chest closet, which opened toward the door behind which he stood, repentant. But no sooner than I regretted my intrusive carelessness in not closing the closet door, he entered the room. I heard the *bump* and then the silence, into which I plummeted in freefall. I knew from the sound that he had bumped his head and I hoped he hadn't put his eye out on the sharp shaped corner. It was bad enough but he said nothing, and after that pause, he came on to the bed. He stood there a moment; even in the dark I could tell that he didn't know how to implore, what position to assume. I didn't help him; I didn't turn on the bedlight; I didn't want to see. I was still plummeting, though his footsteps had given me some purchase on time and space again. He got into bed, embraced me. "I'm sorry," he said, and I wept. "It's o.k." I said, and hoped that it was, but it wasn't. He lay there with me some time longer—I don't know how long; it could have been most of the night—then got up and walked carefully back to his bed: I knew his arms were outstretched to find the cedar chest before it found him; I still would not turn on the light. Next morning there was a spot of blood on my pajamas and one on my pillowcase, brown and accusing; he had a small bandaid on his forehead. We never spoke of the incident, and it has never been more than a thought or two away from my mind. The apology is constant because it was sealed in blood that I had inadvertently (the story of my life: inadvertence) drawn. The affront is there to explain the apology and if the incident had not been significant enough in his own life for him to apologize for it, actually to recognize and admit culpability, doubtless I would have swallowed it too, deep-sixed it too, like everything else.

Still, it's not the apology but his virtually helpless sputtering exasperation at me for walking home, his sense that my walking home was somehow a public humiliation of him, an action that somehow excluded him from a class to which he desperately wanted to belong, that is the subject of this work, the center around which all my memories cohere, the vortex out of which all my meditations about things southern whirl, in double and triple helixes.

i i i.

My father was probably less interested in starting something than in escaping: the starting up of the new was the necessary adjunct to escaping the old, but incidental to it. He had no discernible interest in his origins. If he knew his grandparents he seldom shared them with me, had no pictures of them, no artifacts at all that I knew of. When he talked about his childhood it was neither with pleasure nor with pride or shame either but with a kind of synergetic detachment, as if the kid he was had been somebody else, in another life—which indeed he had been. Of course it may have only seemed that way. My children are not particularly interested in my childhood and I certainly don't overtax them with their family history, partly because I don't know much of it, partly because like all children they get easily and naturally bored with ancestors who did little more than provide the biology and the chemicals for their own complicated synergies and partly because there hasn't seemed to be a natural time to do it. It may well be that my father's reticence was rather my own tin historical ear, which rebelled against him not ever through open defiance of his temper and his will but by a muted resistance to his story: by closing off, refusing to hear, the stories by which he may have hoped to explain, justify himself, if he ever thought justification necessary.

I suspect that in most ways he was not unlike other sons and fathers and husbands of his time and place and no more extraordinary as a random representative of his time and place than his time and place themselves were, even though indubitably southern. Most of my problems with him have nothing to do with southernness at all but rather with more archetypal problems inherent in family structures that Freud and other fiction writers have described. Since we didn't have a "traditional" southern family, most of what I know about extended families and about rural life in the South I know from my reading.

Although I made many forays into rural south Mississippi to deliver merchandise, my relationship to the rural on such trips was an economic one and that of an observer; I stayed no longer than necessary to conduct my business. My actual experience of rural life, as resident alien, was minimal; I gained it on trips to visit those branches of my parents' families that remained more or less in the country, for a time, while nearly all of their siblings found their ways into more urban lives. Visits to the country were always mildly disruptive of my equanimity, and they furnish me with the most traditionally "southern" of my memories.

Except for my mother's mother, I barely remember my grandparents, much less their parents. I have read the standard genealogies and have traced the American Polks from our probably Scottish origins as Pollocks into Pennsylvania and North Carolina in the early nineteenth century. My father's grandfather was Benjamin Franklin Polk, a farmer and part-time logger who flourished in the late nineteenth century; I cannot trace him to any of the Polks of the early part of that century: I lack a generation or two that would connect me directly to those Pollocks and to the dashing Revolutionary War Polks of North Carolina's Mecklenburg County. I own one picture of Benjamin Franklin and his family, taken about 1895. There are nine children (two more were to come later); Ben holds my grandfather, Zebulon Aaron, about five or six, on his knee. It is a period photograph, clearly a formal occasion, and they are all deadly serious: all their eyes, even the infants', are shadowy as they stare at the camera, darkly suspicious of its power; there's not a smile among them. When I look hard I can see myself, I think, in the shape of my grandfather's head, the cut and color of the hair, perhaps in the mouth and chin. I remember my father's Uncle Charles, who was not even born until after this picture was taken, and I have heard stories about Uncle Luke and Uncle Ted; otherwise they remain unknown to me, as do their children and grandchildren, although I have encountered them on occasion. But for the most part my knowledge of either side of my family is not the vertical one of genealogy but the horizontal one of aunts and uncles and first cousins, a large but even so fairly closed and limited group, and I do not know many outside that circle.

My father's brothers and sisters also got the hell out of the country as soon as they could, or if they continued to live in or near the country at least found both jobs that kept them from being dependent on the soil, and transportation that made towns easy to reach; some continued to plant small vegetable gardens and took annual pride in their peas but none depended on planting for their livelihood. Only Virgie, his older sister, stayed in the country. She was a kindly but always harried country woman whose primary duties seemed to be cooking and cleaning and caring for a husband and four children, including Ben, who had multiple sclerosis and had to be tended every minute. Rufus, her husband, was a dairy farmer whom I mostly remember as a barefoot unshaven grizzled man in overalls and no shirt. He was physically so much like what I imagine Faulkner's Anse Bundren to look like that I'm probably imposing Anse on him backward; more likely, since Rufus came first in my experience, I have rather visually imposed him on Anse. Virgie died a most depressing and painful death from bone cancer when I was about twelve; I recall some ghastly visits to her hospital room in Gulfport. I am haunted by the slow laborious process of her dying; she was consumed by pain so long unbearable as to have sucked her spirit and flesh into it:

even as I watched, her gaunt face shrank and her eyes retreated further and further into her skull as though seeking some ragged remnant of flesh or spirit to attach seeing to.

We drove to their house over dirt roads; when it had rained, my father would sometimes stop to let my brother and me wade where the ditches had overflowed low places in the road. Virgie and Rufus lived in a house made of concrete blocks that stood across a dirt, then finally paved, road from the field where their dairy cattle pastured; the dairy was at the other end of the pasture, a most interesting place to visit, and I was pleased to be able to milk a cow. The pasture was a frightening open space because, I was told, there was a bull there. Their back door opened almost directly on to the wilderness.

I spent some happy hours there, revelling in the astonishing amounts of food that Virgie cooked and kept covered on the kitchen table: fresh-churned buttermilk, fried chicken, ham, and fresh-grown vegetables in seemingly endless quantities, sitting there, almost humming, at the beck and call of the appetites of the five men Virgie fed and served. For a week or so every summer I would stay there to play with my cousin Larry, my age and a river rat, a country mouse if there ever was one; he would then come to Picayune for a few days to see how city mice lived. Ben was an enigma to me, fascinating and a little awesome; I was torn between pity and utter admiration. Lying or sitting still, he was constantly in motion because of the multiple sclerosis; immobile, he radiated energy and good will from an infectious grimace of a smile that must have taken a lot of effort and from eyes in which lurked a certainty of some joke that God had played on us and not on him. He spoke in long painful syllables; I never understood a word he said, although Virgie and Rufus seemed to. He loved the Grand Ole Opry, never missed a broadcast; he had a picture of himself with Little Jimmy Dickens that Dickens had signed for him; incredibly, he could actually pick out some tunes with his toes on a cheap guitar.

Austin became a dentist, moved to Dallas and got rich, the only one of the siblings to do so, and was a silent partner in the Firestone Store. We spent most family vacations—vacation defined as those trips away from home for more than one night—usually visiting them in the big city: tall buildings, freeways, shopping centers, jet airliners to watch land and take off at Love Field and, less than an hour away, real cowboys in Fort Worth. It was a clamorously wonderful place to visit for a small-city boy and I often also exchanged visits with my three cousins there too—no scary open places for bulls to lurk, menacing. Herbert was and remains a river rat who would rather fish than just about anything else; he worked for my father in the Firestone store for a time, then moved to Purvis, on the Black Creek.

Alton wanted nothing more than to be a country musician and did in fact have his own band at various times during his life; in the early fifties he was a disk jockey at a country music station in Arkansas. But mostly he followed my grandfather's calling and became a preacher, settling at last to preach at a small church in Nicholson, just outside Picayune, in the community where his father, my grandfather, had come to preach, drawing his children to the area behind him in his wake. My favorite aunt, Virginia, the baby of the family, dabbled in painting and became a maker of gorgeous quilts; she moved to Picayune, too, and married a wonderfully-dispositioned good-ole-boy *par excellence* named T. J., Thomas John, Shaw, a fourth or fifth cousin of Rufus. I have hardly ever known a sweeter, more congenial, less pretentious person in my life, one less apparently troubled by the world and its complexities; he once taught Dale Carnegie some lessons in how to win friends but never worried overmuch about influencing people. He, too, worked as a clerk in Schrock's Western Auto, then for a while for my father at the Firestone Store. For as long as I have had children he has been the candy truck man, a job that has endeared him to them and to me.

I know even less about the Hamiltons and McDaniels of my mother's antecedents than about the Polks, though there is apparently some chance that I am distantly related to Alexander Hamilton. My mother is from the same southwest Mississippi county my father was, though her family moved around a good bit more, apparently, as her father looked for work lumbering. Far less driven than my father, she provided a constant stable sweet-tempered but, most important to my own stability, predictable counterpoint to his emotional volatility that kept things in our family in better balance than we might otherwise have had. When my father died in 1968 she tried to keep the Firestone Store going for my college-age brother to inherit and come home to, and they worked it together until the mid-seventies when, for a variety of reasons, they closed it and she moved to Hattiesburg to help raise my children; her life with us in Hattiesburg for nearly twenty years now is the limit of the "extended" southern families that I have experienced.

Her mother is the only grandparent I really knew, though I have vague memories of both parents' fathers. She lived to be eighty-four, died when I was in my early thirties, and lived all of her life, at least the part that I knew, on the road. We never went "to Grandma's house" for Christmas or Thanksgiving because when I knew her she didn't have a house of her own. She was an itinerant grandmother, always on call, ready to come and help whenever there was sickness or emergency or any kind of need, but mostly she came and went among us at her own whim. She travelled with whatever family member or friend happened to be driving in whatever direction she wanted to go or maybe, more simply, she always wanted to go and would go in whatever direction she found a car heading, to stay for indefinite periods with each of her children and their families. Even at her age she did more than her share of the household work, cooked wonderfully tasty greasy meals and cakes and pies galore. She spent her leisure time watching soap operas and professional wrestling on television. Although she carried a huge Bible with her wherever she went and read it constantly, she would not go to church with us, she said, because she had left her hat at the last place she had stayed. So far as I'm aware she carried everything she owned, including her Bible, in a single suitcase about the size of a breadbox. She came and stayed and became part of our family without seeming to crowd or take up any extra space; she left without leaving any gap.

Mother had four siblings, Lillian, Champ, Archie, and Ila; Champ and Archie became mechanics, and Ila married one, as did Mother, though that was incidental to my father's larger goals. Lillian married a railroad man. I knew Mother's family generally less well than my father's people primarily because most of my father's folks moved, as he did, to the Picayune area. We therefore had to drive for an hour or more to visit Mother's family in and around Columbia and Monticello, so we spent less time with them, on the whole, except for Lillian, my mother's older sister, a sort of second mother to her, who lived in Columbia or, more properly, out from Columbia in Cheraw, which was itself out from Foxworth. Her husband, Davis, was a rough-hewn leather-skinned railroad man. We made plenty of trips to "Columbia," as we said, though we meant Cheraw. I actually spent a lot of time in Lillian's and Davis's home, especially when Mother and I lived there from 1944–45 while my father was wresting Italy from the Germans and while Mother worked in a parachute factory in Columbia. My actual earliest memory is of playing on the bed with my Aunt Ila's son Tommy, in a cold room with dark unpainted boards for walls, or perhaps it was aging and discolored wallpaper, and a single naked bulb hanging on a long electric cord from the middle of the high ceiling. Tommy and I were bouncing up and down. Perhaps it was morning and we had just waked up, perhaps night and we were over-active; I was no more than two years old; we were jumping and Mother came through the door from the warm bright kitchen, laughing, and maybe even playing with us; Lillian and her daughter Dorothy were in the door, laughing too. That's all—a flash, an image, and nothing more.

Lillian and Davis lived in a large house with a huge front porch protected by huge chinaberry and pecan trees. It was set on a side road that veered off the main highway and ran parallel to it for about a half mile or so into and through their neighborhood of two or three houses, crossed a delicious little creek over an iron bridge that my cousins and I used as a diving platform, then rejoined the highway. From the front porch you could see across the dirt road, across a fenced pasture, to the highway, maybe a couple of hundred yards. On the other side of the highway was a little country store, a combination gas station and grocery, the equivalent of our modern 7–11s, to which we would often go for—yep, Moon Pies, though not an RC Cola but a Double Cola, a concoction that nobody else I've ever talked to has ever heard of; it must have been a local product.

There was country fun to be had in Cheraw. My cousins Bobby, Jim, and Davis Jr., or "Dazzy"—most of my cousins, in fact—were older than I, almost of another generation, and always busy with their own teenager activities, though they were always friendly, always charming, always interested, and always intimidatingly *physical*, somehow: loud and raucous, wrestling and tumbling and laughing all the time and as I thought perfectly at home in the world, as I was not, wherever they happened to be, as were all of my cousins when we would gather at Lillian's for one of those extended southern family get-togethers of a weekend or a Sunday afternoon.

Chickens ran loose in Lillian's small back yard—fearsome awkward nervous creatures that she caught and cooked and that made ventures into the back yard a serious business for me—and an occasional turkey would absolutely petrify me; I remember a mule that I would occasionally risk petting. The back yard separated the house from a huge plot of ground planted in corn and other crops so high it was only slightly less sinister and forbidding than the forest itself at the garden's other side. I never knew whether it was my kinfolks' garden or a neighbor's. The crops encroached on their back yard, a space already crowded by a huge butane tank and a little shed where they housed the electric water pump that kicked on loudly whenever the pressure got too low. In Cheraw I learned from my cousins not about corn and crops, but about snakes and spiders and lizards and praying mantises (don't let them spit tobacco in your eye): useful information for anybody to have and essential for a country boy but not likely to make a city boy feel any more at ease outdoors with his shoes off or his eyes open. I feared the bull in the pasture that my cousins teased me about (I began to assume that bulls inhabited all open spaces in the country), though I never saw it, despite nervously crossing that pasture dozens of times in quest of a Double Cola.

Though our parents expressly forbade us to swim in the little creek up the road without some adult present, it was just far enough away from the house that they couldn't hear us splash and so of course we skinny-dipped whenever we wanted to (I naturally fearful of being discovered), in whatever numbers or combinations of boys and girls we found ourselves in; we stashed our clothes under the iron bridge and waited there to dry before dressing and returning to the house. The creek was nearly ice cold; it was as clear as a mountain stream and had a white smooth sandy bottom, which alone made it possible for me to swim in it, otherwise I could not have. I was a city boy; I swam in the YMCA's concrete pool, whose bottom you could see held no foreign objects, no surprises of sand or rock, eel, gar, or shark. I did not, and still do not, like to swim in oceans or ponds or creeks whose dark surfaces belie the fearsome snag or snake lurking just underneath.

And although clearly we spent a lot of summer time there, else we could not have swum so much, my main memories of Cheraw are of being almost constantly cold: of unused rooms closed off from the heat; of used rooms heated by woodburning fireplaces; of the eternal wait in the mornings for the fireplaces to generate enough heat for comfort, although for me they never seemed to, except up close to the hearth, where it was intolerably hot. The heat never seemed to get beyond the circle of people sitting and standing around it, much less to the dark corners where the single bulb could not throw light. The cold seemed to hide in those corners, storing its own considerable energy and draining the heat from the middle distances of the room. I did not like being inside the circle, near the hearth's heat, so I was constantly cold. Lillian and my grandmother often stood backed up to fireplaces, their dresses hiked up to warm their backsides: I don't remember that my mother ever did that. Cheraw was for me primarily cold, and it was not home. It was not exactly chaos, and it had its charms, but it was close enough to disorder, dis-comfort, to make me constantly wary. It was the country, not the city; bulls and turkeys and nervous chickens lurked in every open space and praying mantises hid in the closed ones, camouflaged and prepared to spit in my eye. It was not home but somewhere else, large and sprawling and uncontained.

Nearly all my parents' siblings moved to town, nearly all downsized their families when they did so. I am now reasonably comfortable with all members of my family within the circle of aunts, uncles, and first cousins, but with few exceptions I am mostly at sea outside that immediacy, and at reunions I struggle with halfremembered names or faces or occasions that come to me in fragments from years and years ago that I can't reassemble into anything like a coherent memory. I don't see my relatives very much any more except at funerals, even though most of us live within a range of a few blocks to seventy-five or a hundred miles and more from each other (some are now in Texas, California, Ohio, and Yemen). I generally don't know my cousins' children very well, or the families of my aunts' and uncles' in-laws, nor they mine.

Our lack of visitation, of complicity in each others' lives, is a natural function of our divergent interests and locations, if not of our preferences. I do not know what they do or how often they visit and interact with each other outside my ken, though we all talk about how infrequently we see each other, and what a shame. Some, I am told, are intimidated by my education and my life as a *professor*, and I do not know how that fact works to include or exclude me from the general chemistry, the specific energy, of family relations. I always worry that the distances between us, and I don't mean miles, will make conversation sustainable for the duration of a funeral but not much longer, and I am always mildly surprised and very pleased when on such occasions my cousins and I find grooves to slip into, rhythms for visiting and catching up in which we seem comfortable, at ease. We make solemn vows to get together more often, but never do. We wait for someone else to die.

When my Polk grandparents were moving to Picayune, my grandmother put the suitcase holding all the family photos and other mementoes on top of the car; the suitcase fell off as they turned one or another bend on the way. Gasoline was very expensive, and they were very poor, so they did not turn around to look for the lost suitcase when they discovered the loss: they kept moving forward, or at least outward. I suspect my family has lost lots of pictures on the various radii they have travelled and have likewise wasted little time in search or in regret. Their memories are the most substantial documentation we have of our past, and to a large extent it is a collective memory of things they—my father, at any rate—didn't talk about to me and perhaps didn't want to have to think about.

iv.

Thus my family history, though totally southern, runs at some odds with the family of the southern "tradition," with its vertical, totemic, enshrinement of origins, its gratifications in the worship of the overlapping generations, the solidity of its roots and trunk, the flowering and complicating interlocking branches of blood relationships. My family history is a history of some dysfunction, of lots of discontinuities: of fragmentation, of diffusion, of scattering, of separation, of elliptical orbits in motion around a center that will not stay put. Above all, at least for my father, it is a history of a flight from, a repudiation of, his origins in rural Mississippi, origins that he hated and never sentimentalized.

Doubtless things would have been different had he lived longer. He was in a real sense the patriarch, even if by default, of both his and my mother's families, at least to the extent that he provided a functional center to which everybody could tether themselves. He made Picayune a geographical and spiritual point of reference, a kind of crossroads if not a home, for everybody; it was not where everybody was *from* but merely where they came whenever they needed to touch base with some remnant of home. When he died the families went eccentric; there was no center to hold or to hold to.

I take the analogy between him and Flem Snopes quite seriously, though of course the analogy goes only so far, since Flem is a fictional construct of a southern type and my father a good deal more complicated. Perhaps it is better—it's certainly more narratively interesting—to have in your past an outrageous figure like the great-grandfather horsethief and reprobate whose dubious accomplishments you tell about from the remove of several generations, with bemused moral detachment, especially if you are enjoying the benefits of the money he made in his renegadery. Certainly a brooding looming tragic figure like Thomas Sutpen, whom you can exorcise in telling about him, whom you can hate and repudiate even while understanding him, is in all kinds of ways a more interesting figure than Flem, whose primary goal in life is to fit in, to be respectable and colorless even in what he would have called success—though to be sure Thomas Sutpen's children don't conspire to have their father killed and Flem Snopes's daughter does. My father is not so easily disposed of as either Sutpen or Flem.

It is quite unfair to him and to the other southern boys of his generation that he here represents to impose Flem's bourgeois emptiness on them. Flem's emptiness, at any rate, is Faulkner's emptiness, an emptiness not of the bourgeois experience but of an intellectual's critique of material culture, the disillusioned intellectual's revenge upon the middleclass. It is easy enough, patronizing enough, to say that the unexamined life is not worth living. But who is to say that my father could not have been, should not have been, happy fitting in, getting along, making his mark in a Babbit-world? And who can say without shame that the middleclass life he aspired to and mostly attained was not, is not, better in all respects than the grinding poverty of the rural life he came from? Let us now praise famous men indeed, but let us not praise them famous by sentimentalizing them out of the circumstances that their lives forced them to function in or against, or patronize them for wanting a part of America's material culture that most intellectuals can be critical of precisely because they can take indoor plumbing for granted.

I have only my own wounds to suggest that my father was not as "happy" as he might have been, especially during my early life, but I am pretty sure that any unhappiness he felt was rooted in childhood and wartime experiences and not in the emptiness of the material culture he was courting. I do not know whether his increased material success in the years preceding his death made him a happy man; I rather suspect it did, and I'm reasonably sure that material success was never for him an end in itself. In any case, our differences never had anything to do with his, our, modest material successes, which he proudly accepted as the plateau he had gained by his singular effort and which I unashamedly accepted as a starting point.

A good deal of my continuing problems with him lies in the fact that his untimely death prevented us from facing many issues we might have resolved, though doubtless I was too conditioned by our earlier relationship ever to have put them on the table, and so we might never have talked about them anyway. Thus it suits my analytical nature, my own residual dissatisfactions, to impose some form of emptiness on him, some unhappiness that I need to discover and understand; otherwise I am left where I started, confronting his dissatisfaction with me.

He left me with a more complex legacy of repulsions and attractions, centrifugal and centripetal, than Sutpen and Flem left. I never wanted to kill him but I often wished him dead, and I don't want to romanticize him as either better or worse than he was. This is no Telemachiad; I am not trying to find him, but rather in important ways trying to lose him, to free either him of me or me of him, or at least to find a place for both of us to let it rest. Like him I am in certain measure escaping my origins, though I've tried to understand my origins in order to exorcise them, while he, so far as I could tell, simply faced forward, always forward.

My own history, then, like a lot of southern history, certainly like southern family chronicles, is less a search for antecedents than a tracing of pathologies, in infinite regression up or down the genetic tree, all the way back to the original family, the Original Fault itself if need be: where did things go wrong? whose fault was it? and how, thirty years and more later, to fix it?

He died in 1968. He had spent the late morning hours out back of the store changing a huge truck tire in the hot July sun. He had lunch, spent the afternoon complaining of indigestion, took his usual Bromo- and Alka-Seltzers and nothing seemed to help. He went home in the evening to the modern brick ranch-style house in the slightly more upscale neighborhood that he and Mother had recently bought. They were to go out that night, and he lay down on the floor in front of the television, to rest a bit while Mother cooked supper. Almost immediately his face turned purple, Mother said, and he was gone. I was away in graduate school. For some reason I've never understood, no one from the family called me directly; a friend called the University of South Carolina's dean of students, who called me with the news. My wife and I flew to New Orleans, were met by relatives, and drove to Picayune.

At the time, I was dry from the combination of grief and relief I felt at his death. I came close to tears only once, during Hoyt Nelson's eulogy, when he talked about my father's frequent generosity to him, as he was preparing for the ministry: a free set of tires here, other things there. I stifled the tears immediately by going analytical: given all the big things, why had such a small one triggered the impulse to weep?

Many in Picayune will remember him as a generous man, and indeed in all material senses he was very generous to me too. He was curiously non-possessive: he never, for example, referred to *his* car or *his* house, but to *our*, the family's, car or house which we shared equally as partners. I hardly wanted for anything that was within our scope, and he and Mother made some sacrifices, I know, to buy my brother and me trumpets when we joined the band and to support us financially when the band travelled; at the same time, he didn't just *give* me things. He also taught me responsibility by allowing me to buy things on the installment plan out of the store, for example, and I was happy, perhaps too happy, to be responsible. I can recount many other acts of kindness and generosity of spirit, offered to relatives and to others who were not as close to him as I was, and to me as I got older and lived elsewhere than in Picayune.

I never doubted that in his own way he loved me too, but his love was always on his terms and he made it my terrifying responsibility to figure out how and when to tap that love, how to be worthy of his generosity. Still, he did the best he could, within his lights, and as I say he was often generous and supportive, even if hardly ever tender and gentle, intimate. I could just never tell which father was going to greet me each day, could never tell what inadvertence, what circumstance from a day or a week ago would bring censure or praise. How much of our problems are traceable to character, mine or his, how much of it his debilitating brushes with vulnerability during the War or on that cold service station floor, how much of it he brought with him from his relationship with his parents, I do not know. It breaks my heart to realize that knowing is hardly to the point any more: when I got old enough to understand that the problem might rather be in him than in me, he was long since dead. Even so, even knowing, I have spent hours of psychic energy trying to understand him, trying to figure out what was wrong with him, to fix *him* somehow, even in my memory, to make everything retroactively all right.

I could never fix on either love or hate as the controlling, single clean uncomplicated purgative emotion in our relationship. Nor did I understand, then, that it was possible to own both emotions at the same time; one could exist only at the expense of the other. How much better if I had known how to be angry even in love, how to let myself explode too; how much better to have learned that from his example. His anger, his volatility, held me hostage; it always took advantage of my need. And that's it, the problem with anger, whatever its sources: its unfair advantage. Even when it's not exploding it's always lying there like a land mine, forcing you to be always conscious of where you step. He would blow up in anger in a moment and be over it instantly, calm and equable and charming again. Like every bad-tempered person I have ever known, he always claimed that those explosions were healthy. I can testify that they are healthier for the exploder than for the hapless victims of the blowup, even for the innocent bystanders who get caught in the incidental shrapnel.

In my more generous moods I can indeed think of him as wanting something I might eventually have been able to give him had he lived long enough. He often said, and I believed, that he wanted us to have things he didn't have, and I know that he didn't mean just material things. Perhaps we missed each other simply because my need caught him at a time when he had to concentrate on the material side of his ambition, but I think it's far more complicated than that: in order to provide me those things he had not had he necessarily positioned me, as a city boy, to be able to want things that he, as a country boy, could not have wanted because he didn't know they were there to be wanted. We thus wound up wanting different things, things which might have been compatible had he lived long enough for us to reconcile them.

He manifestly wanted me to succeed and to be happy and productive, took pride in the little I accomplished before he died. What I wanted was not in him to give or to accept, probably not in me to articulate in any way that either of us at the time could have understood. I am sure that he knew then, as I was to learn only later, that to need is to be vulnerable. So far as I could tell, he did not need from me either understanding or any form of love that I could have described: respect and obedience were as close as either of us could have come. I therefore insulated myself from him and his volatility by withholding my love. I am now no more permeable to love or hate than forty years ago. He beat them out of me, or perhaps rather drove them indelibly inward. Perhaps he did this deliberately, even if not consciously; perhaps he was protecting himself, too, from vulnerability: from my love, by quashing it in me.

In ways I am still stuck in that darkened room, waiting for another apology, which will never come and which I can't move on without. Mostly now, I don't feel much of anything for him: neither love nor hate, fear nor pity nor pride, pain nor pleasure, not even indifference. When I let myself feel anything, it is not even regret so much as a constant ponderable sadness at whatever of family we didn't have because he had his history and I had mine, he was therefore he and I was therefore I, blood be damned, and because each of us desperately needed the other to be something that he was not and could never be.

The View from Lookout Mountain

Saturday morning, April 25, 1959, I got to the Firestone store around 7:30 or 8. My father was standing in the back with a group of four or five men. I don't remember who they were: no faces or shapes emerge from the general outline, but nobody was unshaven or wearing overalls or straw hats or smoking scraggly self-rolled cigarettes. They were talking among themselves in ways that suggested the topic was something I was not supposed to hear. My radar was always out for things I was excluded from, so I nodded at my father and went about my usual redding up for business of rolling the lawnmowers and the fishing poles out for display on the sidewalk in front of the store, and then sweeping the floor. After some minutes the group dispersed; my father called me back and told me, man to man, in hushed tones though there was nobody else in the store, that the previous night some men had broken in to the county jail at Poplarville, twenty miles to the north, and taken Mack Charles Parker—"that nigger," I'm sure he said, "that raped that pregnant white woman." I'd like to be more certain that he added "and killed him." That's what I remember he said, but I can't be sure. In fact, the police and FBI didn't locate Parker's body for several days after his abduction; the lynchers had thrown it in the Pearl River off of a bridge between Crossroads, Mississippi, and Bogalusa,

Louisiana, and it had worked its way downstream while officials searched the countryside.*

If my father did say "and killed him," he had either just learned something from the men he was talking to, was assuming probabilities, or knew more about the incident than he ever let on—to me—any more directly than that. He knew fairly well at least two of the men involved in the lynching: J. P. Walker, the apparent ringleader of the mob, the only one from Picayune, and Judge Sebe Dale, a virulently segregationist judge from Columbia whose actions from the bench helped to create the climate that allowed Parker's murder to happen. Dale didn't actually go to Poplarville with the mob, but his silence and approval encouraged the men who did. Whether any of the men at the store that morning were involved I do not know. It is of course possible that they were not talking about Parker at all, but were rather telling other kinds of stories they thought young ears should not hear; but I bet they were talking about *it*. Perhaps that is why I can't remember any of them.

---

*The lynching itself bears few of the markers of the racial lynching of the southern stereotype: there was no surly mob fueled by rumors of foul Negro deeds about to go unpunished, as in Faulkner's "That Evening Sun" and *Light in August*, and operating out of some highly public, impassioned impulse to protect our womenfolks or our way of life. The reason for the lynching, according to Howard Smead, was to prevent a trial (though there was in fact a very good chance that Parker would have been convicted) during which black lawyers for Parker would have been allowed to interrogate the white rape victim on the stand.

Though not of the dramatic stereotype, however, Parker's lynching was very much a "classic" lynching: coldblooded and institutional, official, done by and with the cooperation of certain Pearl River County law officers. Given the developing racial climate in the late fifties, it seems apparent that the perpetrators intended to use Parker as a preemptory strike, an object lesson for other local blacks to beware of getting restless or uppity; metaphorically, one might see it as an attempt to insert themselves—us—into "southern history." See Smead, *Blood Justice: The Lynching of Mack Charles Parker* (New York: Oxford University Press, 1986).

At least part of what's at stake for me in remembering this has less to do with my father than with a rather melodramatic, and perhaps manufactured, historical irony in which I associate my hearing the news of Parker's lynching with the almost simultaneous news of the death of the last Civil War veteran. As I remember it, my history teacher, Mrs. Viola Richardson, had announced this fact, with her own heavy square-jawed historical irony, the very day before in American history, even while the perpetrators were making their last-minute plans to abduct Parker. He died, he was a Confederate soldier, he was a Mississippian: "You know what this means?" None of us did, of course, and she could barely contain her mirth: "It means that the South won the Civil War!" Perhaps I've conflated these two events in my mind; I've no idea how close to each other in time or space they actually were, and don't really want to find out, because the conjunction gives me at least a metaphorical fix on southern and Mississippi history of the following decade and a half.

I'm sure I've romanticized that little coffee-klatch meeting that early Saturday morning at the Firestone Store into something that would give me some personal connection to Parker's lynching, some direct association with an actual foul *event* that would give me also at least some claim on the more volatile aspects of the South's racial history, even if only to have been able to tell about it now, or simply to have been haunted by it.

I have been haunted by it: not in nightmares of burning crosses or of bonfires made of exploding churches, as other southerners have been haunted, but rather in a noncombustible, nagging sense of how close I had come, then and subsequently, to "southern history" without actually experiencing it. I'm not sure what I would have done then, or would do now, with more certain knowledge that my father was involved in Parker's lynching. This far removed I am safe in believing that a direct connection would have outraged me, rivetted me into some form of rebellion, would have provided a jump start to a more active rejection of Picayune's racial mores.

The middleaged romantic in me would like for there to have been such a dramatic crisis, such a crystallizing moment in which things would suddenly have clarified themselves and thrown me too into heroic relief against my times. Truth to tell, though, what has niggled and nagged at me all these years is a sense of actual profound relief that in fact I was spared such a terrifying epiphany, and so spared the choice between background and racial justice, the choice others made, suffered for, died for: relief that now forty years later always threatens to reverse on itself and to become regret, accusation that I have to keep constantly at bay.

Close as it was, Parker's lynching didn't happen in Picayune; and even though I now know that my father knew, and I knew them too, at least two of the men involved in the lynching; even though I read about it in the Picayune *Item*, read Chance Cole's incendiary editorials about Parker's just deserts and the just deserts of the black lawyers from the NAACP who would arrogantly insist on a change of venue for Parker's trial and on questioning the white rape victim on the witness stand; even though all this, still the lynching happened twenty miles from Picayune. For me, "southern history"—lynching, violence, turmoil—always happened somewhere else, twenty-five or a hundred or a thousand miles from Picayune or wherever I happened to be, and I remained mostly insulated from it. Except for that small group of men, in our store, the morning after.

I do not believe that my father had anything to do with the lynching, and I do not know what difference it would make to me now to discover that he did or did not participate, that he did or did not have prior knowledge of what was going to happen, that he did or did not try to stop it. Howard Smead's *Blood Justice* does not mention him even by implication, and I am sure that he did not have that kind of violence in him, though I occasionally saw him do things that frightened me into speechlessness at the time. When he went bill-collecting in the quarters, for example, trying to track down black customers who had fallen behind in their monthly or weekly payments for tires or appliances they had bought from us on the installment plan, he would carry a billy-club, prominently stuck in his back pocket. On several occasions I saw him go in to black peoples' houses unannounced, without knocking— to catch them before they ran out the back door, he said—and I have seen him pull the billy-club and charge angrily toward black men who sassed him or seemed indifferent to his demands for his money; just to scare them, he said. He didn't always get money on these sorties, but always got at least promises to pay the next day, or on Friday, or payday. I was astonished then, and I still reel when I think that we—I by his side or trailing at some distance when he moved quickly—were never even challenged, much less harmed or sued, by anybody about our right to do this disgraceful thing, to invade their homes and threaten them with violence. It seemed to be our right, as white and as creditors, to do what was necessary to collect what was owed us, though to be sure I never saw him do this to a white customer, no matter how far in arrears. I assumed my father was angry; I recognized the features. But, back in the pickup truck and on the way home, he would smile and even laugh at the evening's events, certain that there had been no danger. I wasn't so sure. I'm still not.

In fact, our black customers seemed to like my father, seemed to like me—"young Mist' Fi'stone"—and, more, seemed to enjoy congregating in the store of a Friday and Saturday afternoon to get their checks cashed, pay their notes, make purchases, and stand around drinking Cokes and shooting the bull with us and other white and black customers while we changed their tires or prepared the contracts for what they had bought. Amazingly to me, the folks we had visited the night before would often show up, money in hand, as promised, and catch their accounts up with a show of good humor that I then had no doubt was genuine, though it would be naive from this distance not to believe that their good humor was a necessary part of survival. I was a bit shamefaced to see them, uncomfortable. My father was as benevolent and glad to see them as if they were old friends, as though the previous evening had never been; he would even sell them something else, on the installment plan, as though the hunting down, the invasion, the threatening and cajoling, were all part of an economic and social game whose rules everybody understood.

It will thus seem odd, maybe preposterous, for me to claim that in spite of the Mack Charles Parker affair, in spite of such forays into the black community as my father and I made, for the life of me I do not remember life in Picayune—white life, I mean—as having been "dominated" or "overwhelmed" by race, as many argue of the South, or that it was the one inescapable and defining issue, constantly present in our minds. It was certainly there, of course, unavoidable, in our breathing, our language, our educational and cultural curricula, and our values, but I did not *experience* it as pervasive or even particularly intense, although it may seem so when I tell about it here, concentrating a lot of it into a brief space.

I grant that I'm claiming a fine, perhaps a pathetic, distinction, since it was of course its very constancy that kept race from seeming intense, the extent of the pervasiveness that kept it from being even particularly noticeable unless you knew what you were looking at. Its pervasiveness kept it invisible, like the forest and the trees, and therefore much more insidious. The smoothness of its texture provided little purchase for resistance, little friction for rebellion to function against, even had I been capable of resistance. And there were no dramatic episodes in Picayune, like Mack Charles Parker, to render it visible.

I do not claim my experiences as typical or representative. Such claim is, of course, self-protective and assumes the high probability of my blindness to what was going on around me. I absolve myself of having been willfully blind, of deliberately refusing to see race relations then in the same light as I have learned to see them. I am more concerned, four decades and more later, to be absolved of naïveté than of blindness. Although naïveté might somehow let me more easily off the moral hook, it is the less attractive explanation of the history of one who wants to have been more perceptive, and so more critical, of his life and his culture than he was. To have been willfully blind would at least imply some choice in matters, even if it were the choice of cowardice, the choice to invest in the status quo as the only logical alternative to chaos. In short, I want to have had opinions, which I have evaded most of my life, not revelling in controversy or confrontation as some do; I have always tried to assume the morally superior face of reason, of dispassionate interest in all sides of any issue, even in those in which I have been a combatant. This is, of course, a morally evasive position; worse, it is actually no position at all, since its movable, unmoored location between the extremes is dictated by the position of the extremes and not by its own centeredness. Being naive is much worse than being wrong, since wrong can be forgiven or at least corrected. To be, or rather to feel, naive is more morally debilitating even than pride, since naïveté finally, inevitably, recognizes itself. It is the cruellest of the mirrors your own history forces you to look into; it forces you to feed upon yourself: a Medusa that is the mirror itself.

Although I did feel some shame in racial matters, it must have been so diluted with confusion as to be unrecognizable, and I suspect that in thinking about it I've situated shame in my memory as a way of imposing some articulatable order on the chaos of things I felt then and have felt since. Perhaps I merely want there to have been shame; perhaps to discover shame would absolve me of the naïveté, although to be sure it would convict me of cowardice. As I say, I would naturally prefer to write, as others have done, about my growing sense of outrage and my conviction that I had to *do something about it* in order to live with myself, of my courage and my adventures in an activist resistance. But I felt none of those things, until later, safely after the bombs and bullets and the marches.

I did not feel indifference in Picayune, but I did not feel outrage either; given my relationship with my father and my respect for authority in general, I doubt if I knew what outrage was, except as something to be repressed, turned inward. I knew that something was not quite right but, given the regime of assumptions that I grew up with, I was not sure what it was. My actual experiences created lots of dissonances with my assumptions: sympathies furtively aroused by my various encounters with blacks' poverty and economic disfranchisement (which our language described as squalor and chaos) were effectively countered by assumptions that *that was the way they were*, what they preferred. Hence a good deal of confusion, since who could *prefer* to live that way?

i i .

We had no maid nor house servant. Mother once hired a black woman to do some ironing, but I do not know how long she worked for us. She had a baby named Noel, she told me when Mother introduced us—but not named after me, she assured me quickly, as if to head off any reaction I might have had at having a black namesake. I had a reaction anyway, a flicker of panic or concern that was closer to mild embarrassment than to anything else, though it would not actually have been embarrassment unless my friends found out about it and teased me; the teasing would bother me more than the namesake, though neither would have been unbearable. I did not want to be teased about having a "nigger" name: *Noel* was much less common among blacks and whites as a name than John, George, Robert, and James (I knew one other Noel in Picayune, a male, white; the only other one I had ever heard of, save at Christmastime, was the actress Noel Neill, who played Lois Lane on the *Superman* television show), but it was precisely its relative rarity that made me think it so easily expropriatable, somehow tainted or at least taintable.

Picayune blacks lived in what were called "nigger quarters" or, more kindly, simply "the quarters"—Green Quarters, Rosa Street, the "Nigger Project" (there was one federal housing project for whites, one for blacks)—which term, I suppose, was Picayune's only heritage, and that linguistic, from Mississippi's plantation history. Blacks were all neatly separated from the rest of us in three or four definite sections on the outskirts of town; they were thus excluded metaphorically, as geographically and politically, from the center of things. To be sure, some whites did have to pass through or by these quarters on their way from home to town and back, but for the most part if you saw the physical circumstances of their lives up close you had to go there to do it. I went to these "quarters" a good deal on various errands from the store, to deliver merchandise, to retrieve it for repair or repossession.

Many of my friends had black domestic help, servants and cooks who lived in these quarters and had worked for their families for years. Having domestic help put them in a fairly sanitized relationship with Picayune blacks; they saw Negroes, or at least *a* Negro, at their best, as it were, at their happiest, cleanest, most subservient, least threatening, *most civilized*, as we might have put it. So far as I remember, many of my friends' personal experiences of blacks were almost exclusively that in their own homes; I don't believe many had the range of acquaintance with Picayune blacks as I gained working at the store. Those who seemed to entertain some animus about blacks did not, I believe, have such domestic help, probably because they could not afford it; they, watching my own behavior, perhaps not always different from theirs, might well have thought that it was I with the animus.

I laughed when their animus took the form of jokes and took no issue with them, not knowing that there was really anything to take issue with. J. C. David, who lived in Picayune only a few years, coming

there from and going away to God knows where, had a great deal of
fun with tales of how he and a few always unnamed friends had had
a good time over the weekend, say, by putting one of their number in
the trunk of his car, then dousing one arm with catsup and letting it
hang out the trunk as they drove through the quarters, regaling us with
the Negroes' frightened reactions to their certain belief that there was a
murdered white man in the trunk. I never knew whether J. C. was telling
the truth or not, never wanted to have been part of their merry gang. I
doubted that the blacks would have been frightened by such a silly thing;
I assumed they would have been more irritated than anything else.

The janitor at Picayune High was an old bald black man who had
an indentation, a veritable *hole*, on the left side of his head almost the
exact size and shape of the mold you'd use to make the ball of a ball-peen
hammer. One friend had a vast and constantly expanding repertoire of
jokes on this limited subject, most of them revolving rather crudely and
predictably around holes in the head, brains leaking out, and his claim
of having put the hole there with that ball-peen hammer. The jokes were
not themselves racist. His sense of humor was absolutely no respecter
of race, creed, gender, or color, and I have no doubt that had even our
principal, Mr. Skinner, been so endowed, my friend would have made
the same jokes.

Indeed, we all made a great deal of the wonderfully curious circumstance that Mr. *Skinner* was succeeded as principal by Mr. *Slaughter*.
We *all* had a good time with that, and with a physical infirmity that
Mr. Slaughter could help no more than the janitor could help the
hole in his head. Mr. Slaughter had a terrible habit of sniffing between
every phrase, almost between every word he uttered; doubtless he had a
congenital sinus problem, but his *sniffs* were an irritating speech tic, and
when he'd try to address the student body in assembly he could hardly
get through his first sentence before he'd be drowned out by a rousing
chorus of communal sniffing from the students. Teachers were helpless

to stop it; Mr. Slaughter pretended not to notice. Nobody heard a single announcement he made during the years he was our principal.

But there was not the same edge to this treatment of Mr. Slaughter, even so openly, as there was to the jokes about the janitor's head. It was not an edge that any of us could have identified as racist; so far as I am aware nobody ever said anything directly insulting to the janitor. On the other hand, as a group we made raucous fun in public of Mr. Slaughter, loudly and frequently, although of course we would not have done so in a situation where we could be caught individually at it, partly because we didn't want to get punished but mostly, I know, because it was easy to act *en masse* as if he had no feelings and impossible to do so as individuals. We would *never* have acted in such a public way toward the janitor. Thus finally manners, failing toward the white man, prevailed toward the black.

Mrs. Arthur, the mother of one of my good friends, was among the sweetest, kindest people I ever knew. I once watched her feed an old black man who had done some yard work. She prepared—"fixed," all three of us would have said—him a full plate from the meal she was cooking for her family, poured him a glass of iced tea. She handed the meal to him out the back door; he sat down on the back steps and ate, and she chatted amiably with him while she continued the business of getting our lunch ready. When he finished eating, he handed the dishes back to her, thanked her graciously for the fine food. She just as graciously welcomed him to it, to more if he was still hungry. He declined and went back to work to finish whatever he had been doing in the yard. Mrs. Arthur sat his dishes on the kitchen counter; they stayed there the rest of the afternoon. When he finally finished his work and left, she took them—plate, glass, knife, fork, and spoon—outside to the garbage can and discreetly dropped them in. I was ten or twelve. I asked her why she didn't just wash them. I don't remember her answer precisely, but it had something to do with perhaps disease. I thought then that the episode was a lesson in hygiene; I now know it was a lesson, if unintentional, in manners. Mrs. Arthur, like my own mother, would have given him absolutely as much of her food as he could have eaten, and she would have been *very* embarrassed had he seen her throw those dishes away.

I do not hold this episode against Mrs. Arthur, nor tell it now to be critical, because she was not alone, not by a long shot. I know one white Mississippian, nearly twenty years my senior, whose credentials as a racial liberal, even radical, are unimpugnable. In the sixties he signed every petition he could find, marched in every demonstration he could get to, protested every injustice he came upon. He has told me on more than one occasion that during his years as a protester and activist, and even yet, he would cringe slightly when he would go into blacks' homes for meetings and would always have to overcome a certain reluctance even to shake a black hand in greeting. Similarly, my father talked lots about an uprising, about the NAACP as a Communist front and Martin Luther King as a Communist dupe, and worried constantly about the political implications of NAACP activities. But what most exercised him, what most infuriated and frustrated him, what made him feel most helpless, was the rumor that the NAACP had begun paying big money to local Negroes to go into crowded stores and just bump into white people—just *bump into* us, *touch* us: that's all. Clearly, my friend and my father had imbued the same nourishment from the same cultural breast, and I emphatically do not mean just southern culture, that my other friends and I had.

It's that peculiar combination of the instinctive withdrawal from contact on the one hand, which insists powerfully on difference, and on the other hand of manners, forms of learned behavior which insist just as powerfully that there is no difference. That peculiar combination of furious repulsion and cool embracement creates the vicious paradox of noblesse oblige southern style, the dark underbelly of southern manners, maybe of all manners, which allows differences of race and caste and class to exist without a formal acknowledgment of them—or rather, more particularly, without a formal acknowledgment that the differences matter or have anything to do with human interaction. You may not think that there was anything subtle or mannersable about Mrs. Arthur's feeding of the black yard man, but I assure you there was. It's also very much worth noting that a white yard man, one at least that she knew no better than she did this black one, would have gotten almost exactly the same treatment from her—perhaps, though not definitely, to the final disposition of the dishes if she had decided him diseased or unclean; and no more than the black yard man would he have violated the class protocol of their relationship. The difference lay, obviously, in their shared assumptions about purely racial instead of merely class protocols in such social interactions. But clearly there were gender proprieties operating too, and I'd bet that most hired black women—like the woman Mother hired to iron for her—could have sat at table and that Mrs. Arthur, or more likely she, would have washed the dishes for re-use.

One of the assumptions Mrs. Arthur and the yard man shared, of course, was the possible consequence if he should presume upon or in any way violate the protocols. No black person in any part of this country has ever lived without the threat of violence hanging directly overhead, and there was sufficient demonstration of white power in the daily news for both of them to be under no delusions about what kept the assumptions in place and workable, although to be sure Mrs. Arthur would have been horrified even to think that this yard man, eating her food so congenially, might become the victim of a lynch mob; she would certainly have taken no satisfaction in the violence and would have tried to stop it if she could. Violence is untidy, and manners sweep untidiness under the rug. The very niceness of the manners helped perpetuate the ugliness of the racial structures by velvetgloving the possibility of violence—the claw in the paw—so that violence and manners formed a doubly-intricate interlocked whammy. Blacks depended on the niceness of whites and were under considerable operating pressure to be thought of as "good niggers." Culture and religion exhorted everybody, white and black, to return manners with manners, even to return evil with good, though obviously blacks had to be nicer than whites—more elaborately, more exaggeratedly, perhaps even more grotesquely nice—in order for their niceness to be even noticed. By the same token, the protocols required them to ignore whites' bad manners and even to act as though whites' bad manners were good manners: this too a survival technique, part of being a "good nigger." When black violation of any of the protocols resulted in swift retribution, whites could say, with equanimity and with absolute good faith in the protocols, not even "She deserved it for being uppity" but simply, and with genuine surprise in their collective voice, "Why would he do this to us? We were so *nice* to him." A master is always a master, of course; but a nice master is harder to resist than an un-nice one.

I do not know how strongly Picayune blacks felt any immediate or constant threat of violence, since there was no history of gross racial violence in Picayune—or rather, to be specific, little history of actual lynching in the area, since the kinds of billy-club intimidation that my father practiced in his bill-collecting rounds obviously constituted a threat of violence that served the same purpose as lynchings would have, and more neatly. Doubtless Picayune blacks simply didn't "act up" sufficiently to make lynching a "necessity"—or a practical option, at any rate. Indeed, there were no lynchings of black men in Picayune itself, and prior to the Parker murder, in Poplarville, in 1959, the most recent lynching of a black man in Pearl River County was in the mid-twenties. There was rather in fact a considerable history of cooperation and collegiality between working classes of both races—though this, too, may only be because blacks willed it that way out of fear for their safety—that dated from shared experiences, shared labor and wages, in logging camps and sawmills in to and through the Depression when the lumbering industry sagged almost to oblivion and the Crosbys made no distinctions of color among the employees to whom they made available, at no cost, such materials—seed, tools—as they needed to keep alive when there was no income. Because the soil would not support it, south Mississippi did not develop as the Delta did, as a plantation economy. There was an occasional plantation in the area and a scattering of slaves before the war; but what slaves there were mostly worked in logging and on a few small farms.

Because there were no large plantations with large numbers of slaves to run them before the Civil War, south Mississippi after the War did not turn, as the Delta did, to sharecropping or tenant-farming systems that put the majority free black population in direct competition with the minority white population, dirt farmers, for the best plots of land. Sharecropping kept them economically bound not just to the land but, for the most part, to a particular piece of land and to a particular landowner. South Mississippi after the War was not significantly different from before it; the economy was still driven by lumbering and a few free blacks instead of a few slaves worked side by side with whites, though to be sure more whites worked in supervisory capacities and blacks did most of the heavy work. Since they couldn't log where there were no trees, the work was by its nature not bound to one plot of land, but rather constantly mobile; blacks and whites went where the trees were. Mobility was a fact of life until the railroad, various rail spurs, and other forms of improved transportation made more centralized sawmills possible, so that even though the loggers had to chase the trees, the millmen at least could establish some sort of permanency.

Besides Mack Charles Parker, the only other violent death I recall in Picayune was when the city marshal "killed a nigger," as my father put it, in the course of arresting him after a barroom brawl. My father did not report this with any glee or pleasure, and was at some pains to assure me that the marshal himself was terribly upset at having taken a human life, which was a serious, serious business, no matter the color of the deceased or the circumstances of the killing. This is what helps me believe that he did not participate in nor approve of Parker's lynching. According to John Napier, the one lynching in the area was of a white man, not a black one. I technically except the case of Parker. It's a *technical* exception because the lynching took place in Poplarville, about twenty miles north of Picayune and so out of the range of the Picayune "area" I'm considering, even though one Picayune man was directly involved. I don't want to mitigate the brutality or in any way condone the act but merely to suggest that the episode stands out as a gigantic exception in the history of race relations in the Pearl River basin of south Mississippi and is in all kinds of ways as anomalous as a mountain would be in the Delta.

iii.

I insist that I'm not writing about *me*, but I have to get a fix on where I was situated, on what particular lenses I was looking through when I was looking in order to see what I saw and what I didn't. I breathed the same air as my friends, had mannersable parents who raised me in and on my culture, who raised me to have manners. No more than anybody I knew would I have hurt a Negro's, or anybody else's, feelings, or knowingly condescended to anybody. But I did not shrink from the sort of physical contact a handshake or even, occasionally, a hug would have entailed. It would be immoral to claim superiority of any kind, for I clearly was not, am not, morally superior in these things. Perhaps the kindest thing I can say of my attitudes then is that they were somehow tempered, gentled, toward blacks both by my uncertainties about my own place in the world and by some empathy I had gained from dealing with them in a wider range of circumstances than many of my friends did—from blacks' economic and personal worst circumstances in their own homes, where they jousted most intimately, every day, with their poverty, to junctures in our mutual lives where many did, but many others did not, fit the stereotype.

But to claim something as clearcut as sympathy is to overstate the case considerably, and damning, since I did nothing; though to damn myself is to assume that a lone white lower middleclass teenager in fifties Mississippi could have thought his way into and through the racial nightmare of that time and then have *done something*. As I say, in my more heroic fantasies, I know that I *would have* done something if there had been anything to do something about—some fissure in or disruption of the day-to-day fabric, in Picayune, of the sort that seems to have occurred in other parts of the South—an Emmett Till, say—something that would have kicked confusion over into outrage, something about which I could say definitely, This is right, this is wrong. You can't *do something about* the water in which you are swimming; you can only get out of it. But you don't know to get out of it if you don't know you are in it.

Perhaps it was simple disbelief, an unarticulatable refusal to believe that people could live the way many blacks in Picayune lived without being completely content with their lot. Oh yes, I had the temerity, the stunning naïveté, the patronizing arrogance, to believe that if asked black people would give Young Mist' Fi'stone an honest answer about their lives and the outside pressures for change. I believed that I was an earnest seeker after truth, though what I would have done with knowledge that they were in fact miserable in the status quo, I of course do not know. Their responses to my questions, most often asked while I was stripped to the waist and wrestling with the tires they had bought, installing them on their cars, mostly confirmed me in a status quo I wanted to be confirmed in. In college in the early sixties, where change was somewhat harder to escape than at home, I trotted out these "conversations" with Picayune Negroes as proof that I "knew" black people and that critics of the system didn't know what they were talking about.

But I do not believe that all those folks who told me they were content with the status quo were lying, not completely. Oppressed people can sometimes be even more psychologically committed to the ideology that oppresses them than their oppressors are, a horrible truth that gives their oppressors considerable power over them: control the way folks think and you can control the way they live, the demands they are capable of making on you. At some level surely they were as fearful of change as we were, if for different reasons: if they had learned to tolerate their lives, which even *I* knew were at best less agreeable than most poor white people would put up with, what reason had they to hope that change would necessarily be better? Or, more properly, and with perhaps some prescience of the coming storm, what reason had they to think that they, their children, could survive such confrontations as change would necessitate? What sacrifices were they willing to make, individually, for their race?

In college my sense of things became serious questions, which is as it should be, especially as the civil rights movement, the freedom riders, and other assorted assaults on Mississippi were being mounted in Jackson, less than ten miles from where I sat. Professors at Mississippi College like Louis Dollarhide, Joe Cooper, and Plautus and Sue Lipsey gave me some focus for the chaotic store of things I brought with me from Picayune. Mr. Lipsey was monstrously old when I knew him; he had covered the Scopes trial as a young reporter; he talked about how rapaciously the status quo preyed upon unsuspicious, unskeptical minds. Joe had me reading Sartre and Camus and Kierkegaard and Nietzsche. Louis gave me Faulkner, who had not been part of my reading in Picayune. Louis also introduced me to Evans Harrington, at the University of Mississippi, a novelist and short story writer, a long time member of the ACLU, friend and colleague of the rabblerousing Jim Silver, and who had been involved openly, at risk to his employment and even his life, in every radical cause he could get himself to. Barry Hannah was a student at Mississippi College, as were others, like Karolyn Kosanke and Horace Newcomb, DeRoy Johnson, and one philosophy major I remember only as "Soc," a familiar form of his formal nickname "Socrates." All of these, though barely a year older than I, were light years ahead of me in sophistication—what they had read, what they had done, what they had allowed themselves to think—and so they seemed to me at first a little sinister, a little daunting, a little threatening, though we all gradually became friends. I was pleased to be allowed to hang around with them and hoped some of their sophistication would rub off on me, for they made me feel how much catching up I had to do in so many different areas.

Along with them and others, I began sneaking out to Tougaloo College, the black college just outside of Jackson which was, and remains, a sort of central clearing house for social change in Mississippi. White northerners with a passion for social justice or a simple missionary zeal would come there to teach and entertainers came to raise money for various causes; Joan Baez performed once. I do mean *sneaking* out there: we at Mississippi College were expressly forbidden to go to activities at Tougaloo: the danger the authorities feared was by no means just physical. But go we did and I, who at first went just to hear Baez, found myself at the end of these concerts standing, holding hands with black strangers, and singing "We Shall Overcome" at the top of my choiry tenor. Heady stuff, and the world began to sort itself out into rights and wrongs: but the new sorting did not simplify, which—simplification—is neither a property nor an obligation of truth.

Because I went to several of those concerts I got invited to attend one of several workshops on race relations that Tougaloo sponsored during those years. One Saturday morning I went by myself—courageously, I assumed, not knowing what physical or psychological abuse might await me—and met for a morning with a small group of fifteen to twenty black and white students. The first order of business was to arrange ourselves in black-white-black-white seating order, then introduce ourselves: where we were from, what we were doing here, what we hoped to gain from the experience. When my turn came I said something like "I am Noel Polk. I have lived all my life in Picayune, Mississippi. I am here to find out what I can. If my father knew I was here, he'd kill me." I was nervous, trying to be funny. The black student next to me followed; he gave his name, then said: "I have lived all my life in Picayune, Mississippi. I am here to find out what I can. If my father knew I was here, he'd kill me." I looked him full in the face for the first time, startled. He—finally—smiled. The others—finally—laughed. I had known his parents for years; they were as close to middleclass as Picayune blacks could be and had been regular customers at the store. I had delivered merchandise to his house many times, but I had never seen him, to notice him.

It was a terrifying moment, a liberating and defining moment, for a couple of reasons: first, simply that he and I had been so close, yet so far apart; second, and more complicating, the fact that he too was genuinely worried that his parents would find out he was at this meeting and would be upset at him for many of the same reasons as mine would be upset at me. After getting right and wrong sorted into place, I had assumed that only whites would be obstructionist to change, that all blacks, who stood to benefit from social change, were necessarily sympathetic to the movement, were eager to be a part of it.

As I say, I had for most of my life assumed that I "knew" black people, understood them, and had reported to others the conversations in which they had testified to their satisfaction with the status quo; now those assumptions turned upon me with a vengeance. Having learned that they didn't *really* enjoy their present circumstances; having learned that that was not really *the way they were*, I now had to learn that black parents could still support, even if only passively, a status quo that was a constant and unrelenting humiliation, that they had nevertheless learned to survive in it, and that they could be just as worried about the safety of their children in those parlous and confusing times as my parents were;

that they could resist change as earnestly as my parents did, if change, if freedom, had to be bought at the price of the life or limb of one of their own children. There was no more defiance in his eyes than there was in mine; there was no room there for defiance: all the available space had been taken up by temerity, some wonderment, and a good deal of the same fear I felt. We were not enemies, we were not brothers; but we were kin in ways neither of us could possibly have suspected before that meeting.

Thus categories of right and wrong became fluid and shifting, overlapping and intermingling: *much* more complex and complicating and subtle than even Faulkner has depicted.

But all that was still years away from the immediacy of the unchanging, the racially placid waters of white Picayune. And though it remained mostly placid, with scarcely a bubble of discontent breaking the surface, the powers of local containment got more active as pressures from the outside, beginning in 1954, seemed more and more to threaten "our way of life." About the most active threats I recall were the rumors that the janitor at the First Baptist Church, a kindly man, had joined the NAACP. It was not yet active intervention in Mississippi's affairs, but the news, that even we in Picayune could not avoid, of Little Rock, of Autherine Lucy's enrollment at the University of Alabama, of boycotts here and there across the South: all this seemed to augur problems for Mississippi, and the campaign mounted by the Citizens' Council of Mississippi began to reach even Picayune.

At first the Council's campaign was subtle, presenting itself as a warning to white Mississippians to be aware of the enemy's subtlety. It was entirely of a piece with the national anxiety about Communists under every bed, and the warnings, the fears, took ludicrous forms. I well remember a junior high assembly during which a woman from the Citizens' Council came to Picayune to talk to us—to *us*: eighth graders!—about how Communists were infiltrating every aspect of our lives and to warn us that we had to be on guard at every instant against being duped by Communist propaganda. One of the chief means the Communists had of corrupting America was, she said, to make Negroes dissatisfied with things, to force upon unwary white people changes that blacks and Communists but not we, American white people, wanted, changes that would disrupt the American way of life and make us vulnerable to Communist incursion; it was the beginning of the end, she swore, if we were not careful. As Exhibit A in her arsenal of examples of just how subtle the Commies were, she displayed a children's book, written for preschoolers, which told the story of a black bunny who wanted to play with a group of white bunnies instead of with the other black ones. A larger rabbit's intervention forced the white ones to accept the black one. The larger rabbit did this "without a single thought about what the white bunnies wanted," this subtle literary critic announced. This was too subtle even for eighth-graders; we thought she was loony.

i v.

I watched the civil rights movement of the early sixties from the middle of the state, just outside of Jackson at Mississippi College, the provincial, stultifying Hedermansever College of Barry Hannah's first novel, the quasi-autobiographical *Geronimo Rex*; he named his fictional college for the prominent Mississippi family, the Hedermans, that owned and published both Jackson newspapers, the morning *Clarion-Ledger* and the afternoon *Jackson Daily News*. The Hedermans had virtual monopolistic control of central Mississippi's information flow; they certainly had control of its ideological diet and fed it to a ravenous clientele. They were principal contributors to Mississippi's reputation as, in James Silver's phrase, a "closed society." They were also prominent Baptists and huge contributors to Mississippi College. Their influence was everywhere;

those of us who were there in the sixties take some malicious pleasure in
Geronimo Rex.

The Hederman papers, as I entered college in the fall of 1961, gave
me a far more vitriolic portrait of race relations—of the utter perfidy of
Negroes (their ingratitude, among other things) and of the self-righteous
niggerloving outsiders of SNCC and NAACP and various other organizations that presumed to tell "us" how we ought to live with "our"
Negroes—than I had ever gotten in Picayune. I was astonished at the
tone of the discourse, which ranged from purblind fear to blustering rage.
I had grown up outside the scope of the Jackson papers. Picayune, in the
southern part of the state, closer to New Orleans than to Jackson, had had
the benefit of New Orleans media, which offered a considerably more
cosmopolitan worldview than that offered by Jackson's. We shopped and
played and did business in New Orleans, read the *Times-Picayune*, and
beginning in 1949 (when my family got our first television; we were, I
think, among the first in Picayune to do so) we watched WDSU-NBC
television. South Louisiana, to be sure, had its own racial conflicts, and
I had heard the racist language of Leander Perez and others of his ilk,
but as reported in media more moderate than the Jackson papers. I
was rocked by the animus in the Jackson papers, found it unsettling to
discover seething where I had been accustomed to placidity.

Mississippi College was a sort of sieve through which passed, and
some detritus got caught, a fair range of Mississippi's attitudes, somehow
made all the more intense by Mississippi College's self-congratulatory
posture as a "Christian" campus. That is, debaters on both sides of
the issue of race relations appealed equally fruitlessly to the same Bible
in defense of their own positions, as they still do; non-debaters stuck
their heads in the sand, claiming that the church ought to stay out
of politics (!), or took more active roles on one side or the other. One
professor in the political science department, William M. Caskey, taught
racism as a central part of his syllabus and as a running theme in all his

conversations and activities. Since he had no other agenda that I could tell, students got graded more or less on the degree to which they shared, or professed to share, his racial views; students in his classes regularly coaxed a friend of mine, a highly talented artist, into drawing cartoons on the days' events—not-so-subtle cartoons featuring Negroes with apelike features; cartoons directly of a piece with those that the Jackson papers published daily—which they would present to him as illustrations for a class report or simply to see if they could make him laugh. They did.

I read Richard Wright's *Black Boy* and *Native Son*; listened to Louis Dollarhide and others criticize the racial climate; read the papers and listened to gossip as the Mississippi College Board of Trustees met regularly to try to figure out how to confront the issue of integration on our campus; tried to make friends with, or at least be friendly to, a wonderful black man named James, who worked in the student coffee shop; went to chapel one Wednesday morning to hear a viciously anti-Semitic talk by a prominent Baptist; went the next Wednesday to hear Dr. Douglas, one of the older members of the religion faculty, remind us all that Jesus was a Jew. Ross Barnett himself reminded us, in chapel, two or three times of Mississippi's fine traditions. Ross was one of the alumni Mississippi College was proudest of.

At Mississippi College I knew, slightly, Kathy Cappomacchia, later Kathy Ainsworth, who was killed in the summer of 1968 in an FBI ambush in Meridian, Mississippi, as she and a cohort were on their way to bomb a Jewish synagogue; she had a pistol in her purse and loads of explosives in the trunk of the car. She was, to the extent that I knew her, one of the sweetest people I ever talked to, and I was stunned in the summer of 1968 to read the news reports, in the *Clarion-Ledger*, about her secret life: fifth-grade teacher by day, Klan bomber by night.* As an

---

*See Jack Nelson, *Terror in the Night: The Klan's Campaign Against the Jews* (New York: Simon & Schuster, 1993).

alumnus, two years removed from the campus physically and by 1968 light years removed ideologically, I was also humiliated and outraged but not really surprised to read *Clarion-Ledger* editorials praising Kathy's activities as an outstanding Christian woman and absolutely glorying in Mississippi College's role in helping produce such fine upstanding young people. Mississippi College made no public attempt that I am aware of to repudiate the *Clarion-Ledger*'s praise. Nearly thirty later these editorials are still hard for me to believe.

At Mississippi College I also knew, also slightly, three of the He-derman children, including Rea, who in the seventies became editor and publisher of the family's newspaper empire. Almost singlehandedly Rea wrecked the family's ideological machine by abandoning the papers' traditional racist monologues, by hiring bright young investigative re-porters from journalism schools in the North and the Midwest to come to Mississippi and ferret out corruption in high and low places. Rea and these reporters brought the *Clarion-Ledger* an almost instant reputation as a first-rate news service; it won several prizes, including at least one Pulitzer. Almost to the degree that his family had held Mississippi as an ideological fiefdom, Rea freed it, or gave it the opportunity to free itself, by providing it with real information.

Mississippi College provided me with my usual vantage just outside the action. I was on the periphery of things, mostly by choice: a craven fear of large crowds that somebody might shoot at. I was never actively involved, not even as a direct observer of all that was happening in Jackson, about seven miles away; so I use the term "watched" loosely. I did my part by being "nice" and by taking home to Picayune a somewhat more liberalized attitude than I had left there with, and with something of a more positive fix on the implications of what was happening in the South than I had had barely a year before. The summer of 1962 was the last I spent in Picayune.

In the early fall of 1962 I watched James Meredith's integration of Ole Miss from my airconditioned dormitory room, followed the controversy during the weeks preceding his advent in Oxford. By the accident of a free ticket, I attended the Ole Miss-Kentucky football game at which Governor Barnett made his infamous speech exhorting resistance, petrified to watch nearly 40,000 people being turned into a lynch mob (all the while, we learned years later, Barnett was negotiating by phone with the Kennedys about how the integration of Ole Miss could proceed with as much facesaving expedition as possible). As confrontation in Oxford became inevitable, Jackson radio stations, especially WJDX, "The Rebel," played "Dixie" continuously; I heard rebel yells all over the Mississippi College campus and I turned down numerous invitations to join the caravan of Mississippi College students who were heading for Oxford. I listened to the blow-by-blow on the radio. On trips home that year I had long serious discussions with my father about the Meredith "situation." He of course blamed Meredith and the NAACP—"Niggers Ain't Acting Like Colored People"—and the Communists for all the violence, and he was livid to read the estimates in the newspapers about how much it was costing the taxpayers *per day* to keep "that nigger" at Ole Miss.

The summer of 1963, when Medgar Evers was murdered in Jackson, I spent working as youth director at a Baptist church in Dallas, Texas, and I read about the shooting in the Dallas *Morning News.* I worked at the church my father's brother Austin attended. Austin had in fact helped arrange the job for me and supported me during the entire summer while I stayed at his house as his guest. I repaid his kindness by helping integrate his church, voting with the pastor and the majority membership on a crucial vote late in the summer. My vote was in all ways a cheap shot: I was a temporary member of the church, a summer employee who had no long-term stake in that church's life but merely in the abstract principle involved. The vote was taken in late summer and so in any case I would not be around to see what effects, if any, integration would have on the church. Though it was of course the "right" thing to do, it was a cowardly substitute for actions I should have been taking closer to home. I could argue with my uncle in ways I could not argue with my father; the cost of disagreement was not so high. To his credit, although we argued about it considerably, and though he was if anything even more resistant to racial change than my father, Austin never reproached me for my vote, never threatened to disown me or kick me out of his house, though I have no doubt that my public opposition must have galled him considerably. Whether—or what—he told my father about the incident I do not know; my father never mentioned it.

The following summer, the climactic summer of 1964, Mississippi's bloody "Freedom Summer," I likewise spent snug and cocooned as a counsellor at a boy's camp on top of Lookout Mountain in northern Alabama, sequestered and remote from even distant repercussion of bomb and bullet—from Schwerner, Goodman, and Cheney.

The symbolism of my position on the mountaintop that summer is too apt for fiction; it would be preposterous in a novel. Yet I in fact, as a southerner, a Mississippian even, inadvertently managed to isolate myself away from what was happening in McComb, Meridian, Jackson, Greenwood, and Philadelphia, managed to be as physically removed from it all as I had been psychologically removed from it in Picayune, the nasty stuff kept at a distance always. Throughout the sixties I never saw a demonstration or a sit-in, never saw even the aftermath of a bombed church, never saw a burning cross—though I once visited the home of a Jewish couple in Jackson who had taken the cross the Klan had burned on their lawn, varnished it for preservation and placed it on their hearth, a macabre and unavoidable centerpiece for their living room, perhaps for their lives. The closest I came to an actual encounter with the Klan, at least that I knew about, was when I moved back to Mississippi in 1977 and I saw a few pathetic remnants of them at highway intersections in Gulfport and Hattiesburg, robed but not masked, handing out political leaflets, their racism only slightly veiled behind the more acceptable codes and phrases of political conservatism and fundamentalism, asking for contributions to save America from moral degeneration.

v.

I thus missed most of southern racial history, though a good deal of it happened within walking distance from where I stood. By my definition, of course, nearly all of the South "missed" southern history; but that too is part of my larger point. "Southern history" gets understandably defined by the signifying confrontations on battlefield or Main Street, not by the quotidian realities. Southern history is larger than, if not so dramatic as, "southern history." I was mostly conscious of being glad to miss "southern history," relieved that the violently changing times didn't call me out, force me to life or death choices that might have left me dead in the middle of the historical road; as the violence and confrontation waned it became easier and easier to be comfortable with the civil rights movement's high idealism, to be openly indignant toward racial injustice. Like Picayune, I and "southern history" ran along side by side in parallel universes, with only occasional genuflections in the other's direction: glances, looks, soft touches because of which we caromed off of each other and went our separate ways.

But "southern history" has caught up with me, and with a vengeance. Its ever-lengthening tail, jerked sharply up by the residual power of the conditions that created so many of the southern and Mississippi stereotypes, almost daily curls and cracks like a bullwhip against the frail skin of my white equanimity, as it becomes more and more obvious both how much and how little change the sixties effected, how little the high idealism of those years could have predicted the direction that race relations have now taken, in Mississippi and in the United States: the increasing distance between the races on campus, for example, the increasingly vocal demands by African Americans for separate educational facilities at the college level.

I am a teacher, a professor. I make my living at a university, in a fairly rarified white atmosphere of mostly rational discourse and reasoned temperaments and a virtually monolithic ideological unanimity about racial and other political matters. It's not exactly Lookout Mountain, but the metaphor is workable, even to the mountain's name and my position atop it during Freedom Summer. Moreover, I live in a world and follow a profession that makes moral posturing not only possible but necessary. I preach wisdom from the Mount when the multitudes come, to the ones that listen and can hear; but then they disperse back to the less rarified air of their lives on the plains where the friction is, where the consequences are. I stay on the mountain, mostly. I talk to them about abortion without ever having to perform one; about euthanasia as an important issue, an ethically provocative abstraction, without much chance of being called upon to perform it; about business and political ethics without having to make business or political decisions. And about race.

I teach Faulkner's *Light in August, Absalom, Absalom!,* and *Go Down, Moses,* and Richard Wright's *Black Boy* and *Native Son* with a great deal of pride and pleasure in how well I understand them, how skillfully I can lead my students to understand the implications of these books' depictions of southern and American race relations. I hope to touch them, somehow, with my own late sixties- and seventies-generated dreams of how race relations ought to be—how far we've come, how far we have yet to go. Yet their experiences in an integrated world are different from mine and I frequently sense that my students simply don't know what I'm talking about—the white ones, I mean; the black ones seem simply to want to get on with it, to cease being called upon to explain. Black and white students worry about their own jobs and futures, which are not so guaranteed as my own professorial sinecure; white students see themselves playing on a field tilted against them; they don't have or want to hear my historical perspective on such matters as, say, affirmative action. They don't understand when black students try to explain how debilitating it is to feel watched when they go in to a department store because someone automatically worries they will steal something. Most don't believe it and the ones that do don't want to hear it. White students just don't get it; and how, indeed, can I pretend to *get it*, standing there in my tenured white skin? No wonder black students have stopped trying to explain, stopped caring whether white students understand or not; no wonder they pull away to themselves.

In a real sense I do live and work not in a professorial ivory tower but at the top of a Lookout. In the ivory tower I'm not expected to be aware of what's going on outside; I'm in fact assumed not to know or care. On the Lookout, however, I'm a sentinel; my job is to keep an eye out for danger. From the Lookout I can see things my students cannot—the broad panorama of race relations, the historical perspective, like a diorama of a Civil War battlefield—and I both deplore the excesses of the past that have created our problems and rail against what I see as the current repetitions of those excesses, rail as a warning against the future. But from the Lookout I can't see the grim curmudgeonry of the daily resistance to change, of life in the trenches, where my children and my students, black and white, have had to live, outside the academy.

Black Mississippians who left their home state in the sixties and seventies and moved back in the eighties have told me that in very many ways race relations are worse now than they were then. Since the evidence of my own experience is that things are immensely better now than thirty years ago, I cannot presume to understand what they mean when they tell me this. But I have heard it too often not to believe that much of the old way lingers, active and resilient, under the surface of political and educational change in the South and everywhere else.

Indeed, on those occasions when I descend from my aerie—to shop, to a dinner party—I'm astonished and bewildered when I encounter fifties and sixties racism: another measure of my continuing naïveté, perhaps. I hear it not just at the garages and the hardware stores but in the homes of doctors and lawyers and, most despisedly, from the highest levels of our government, from our most influential people. Of course they speak the honey-coded words of liberty and justice for all, but the intention behind the words is very clear to anyone who knows what our history is.

I left Picayune long before the integration of the public schools there. My niece and nephew have now graduated from a fully-integrated Picayune High School, as my children have graduated from a fully-integrated Hattiesburg High. We made a point of raising our children without any of the historical baggage that we had grown up with, but their experiences of the daily machinations of race relations, the rubbing, knocking together of equal elbows in the equal school halls, are different from mine in ways I can never appreciate. I meet their tales of friction, of anger, of belligerence, of fear and suspicion, often of threat of danger, first with a skepticism or outright denial born of the sheer will that it were otherwise, then with the stark despair of disappointed hopes, which yields to heartbreak.

We thought it would be better by now. Where I failed my children, where I fail my students, and where I believe my generation failed its own ideals was not in the high white humanism that used "equality" and "equal opportunity" as mantras in a holy war but rather in my failure to teach them the validity, the significance, the dignity of otherness: how to deal with difference. Doubtless we could not have succeeded at this because we did not understand it ourselves. I now know that with all the best intentions what I wanted out of the civil rights movement was not so much equality as absorption, not diversity but unanimity. I wanted to resolve all Problem by a version of the same assimilation that my parents' generation had so feared. I wanted black Americans to *be like me*, or at the very least to accommodate me, so that I wouldn't have to be troubled. I wanted them to change, so that our elbows would move in sync through the halls to *my* rhythm, *my* convenience, which would become their own—as, in fact, it always had been. I believed that, given the chance to be like me, black Americans would leap at it. I thus unwittingly hoped to erase them in the very act of embracing them. I wanted only to embrace an image of myself.

v i .

Southern history has caught up with Picayune too. A couple of years ago it was apparently in a more publicly toxic state of race relations than it has ever been, though obviously I do not know how toxic it was in the black community when I lived there. My nephew and niece witnessed several racial skirmishes at Picayune High, one at least serious enough to necessitate armed guards in the halls for a long cooling-off period. The Klan's Great Kloogle, or whatever the top man in the national organization is called, lived in and operated out of Picayune during much of the eighties.

The Wider World

In 1950 Picayune numbered 6,707 official souls, according to a *Hammond World Atlas* my parents bought, and which I pored over endlessly. We 6,707 were many more than enough to make us statistically and officially a "city," and I was gratified to believe myself a city boy rather than a country boy. This was an important distinction; there was a discernible, identifiable difference between city and country folks—dress, manners, carriage; for girls it was makeup or hairstyle; it may have been the school bus—that made city life seem preferable. I spent hours with the atlas going over and over the populations of cities of the world, mesmerized by the millions in New York and Los Angeles and Hong Kong, disappointed somehow that New Orleans was a long way from the million mark, proud that Picayune was the largest town in Pearl River County at least, and I endlessly compared Picayune's population with other Mississippi towns; I was fixated, for some reason, on our own figure of 6,707.

With the atlas, my parents had also bought a book of photographs of America which contained photos of several American cities, including New York and Chicago and Los Angeles. I fixated manically on these, too, and I was as though transported nightly into those big, wicked, magic cities, without much reason to think I might ever get to one of them, and even with some apprehension at the thought that I might because these were the days when we heard quite regularly about the problem of "juvenile delinquency" in such large places: youth gangs

depicted in *Blackboard Jungle* made those cities seem extremely danger-
ous. At church, the evangelists who claimed some experiences—escape,
survival—of the streets of New York were the ones that thrilled us most.
It was exciting to have survived. Like war, it was somewhere you wanted
to *have been.*

In the sixth grade, Osmond Crosby went to Manhattan with his
parents and not only survived but brought back souvenirs—a one-foot
replica of the Empire State Building, and one of the Statue of Liberty—
to share with us; Oz and Mike Stockstill went to Europe to attend a
Boy Scout Jamboree in Belgium just a few years later and returned with
tales of Paris streets. Otherwise there was no tradition in Picayune to
suggest that I too might travel. I was not particularly jealous of Oz and
Mike, anymore than blue is jealous of red. As I got older I became aware
that students in other parts of the country spent summers backpacking
through Europe: in how many movies did Bobby Darin and various
starlets frolic on the Riviera during their summer vacations? But though
I too wanted to frolic with Sandra Dee on the Riviera, the mechanisms
for getting there, not to say the money, didn't appear to exist, for me, in
Picayune. Besides, the thought of being on my own for a summer was
scary. I was stuck, in Picayune, with the atlas and the census figures.

Then Charlie Newman happened to me. In 1954 Charlie became
director of the Picayune High School band, and changed the name
of the game for me and hundreds of other kids over the next twenty
years. Charlie was an extraordinary blend of Harold Hill, bebop cat,
impresario, and maniac. He was a jazz drummer by avocation and wound
as tight as the head of a snare drum: he not only marched to the beat of
his own drum, he provided the beat for everything he associated with.
He was as full of himself as anybody I have ever known and was always
eager to share the overflow with anybody who would listen—indeed,
even with those who wouldn't. He knew things nobody else knew. He
put a trumpet in my hand and said Blow, boy, and I was never the same.

My piano lessons had fallen victim to baseball and general indolence, but something in the trumpet, which required a mere three fingers instead of ten, lifted me up in to a magical metastate. I was like one suddenly relieved of color blindness and shown thousands of hues and shades and tones and harmonies and patterns in the universe that I had never imagined. It wasn't Sandra Dee, to be sure, but it was frolic, and it was not Picayune's monolithic gray.

Charlie gave me Sousa, of course, and other marchmasters: muscular, rhythmical, and roaring: a release. But mostly he gave me jazz: Stan Kenton's solid astonishing walls of brass and wind, Maynard Ferguson's heartstopping trumpet solos in registers most piccolos could not reach, Carl Fontana's effortless trombone, Lennie Niehaus's breathtaking saxophone, Dizzy's and Miles's smart cool, Brubeck's and Desmond's bliss, Goodman's, Miller's, Herman's frenetic swing, Chet Baker's meditative trumpet and sentimental vocals. Fontana's trombone solos on Kenton's "Intermission Riff" and "Recuerdos" possessed me like benevolent demons. They sang to parts of me that were eons old and I memorized them instantly: they were poems that I have never forgotten and that I still find myself whistling or humming. Even today, hearing them on remastered CDs reduces me to a puddle of transcendence. Every hearing is just as magical as the first: they seem fresh, new, as though Fontana were just making them up, on the spot, every time, just for me.

The music could not be too loud, too brassy, too overpowering, more's the pity for my parents in the other part of the house. I wanted to be enveloped, consumed, intimately pierced in all my parts by every note, to be suspended above the earth, *in* the music, sublimated away into the harmony of the spheres that jazz gave me access to. Even with the serious lack of talent that kept me from being a first-rate musician and the serious lack of discipline that kept me from being even the second-rate one I might have become, music was glorious, otherworldly, and I could be a part of it. I could escape my puritan isolated self by negotiating

one note at a time among a mere three fingers and by buying albums for
$3.98 (stereo, $4.98) in record stores in Hattiesburg and New Orleans!
I took great pleasure in fairly regular trips to the French Quarter to
hear Dixieland at Preservation Hall, to Tulane University for a concert
by the Four Freshmen, and to Hattiesburg to hear two concerts by Stan
Kenton at Mississippi Southern College. On trips to State Band Contest
in Jackson I could spend all my free time in the listening booth at Wright's
Music Store on Capitol Street.

Charlie Newman galvanized Picayune behind the band and took it to
the top of the band world; it was an extraordinary time for a small-
city Mississippi boy. Charlie and music gave me a flashing of rapture,
a community that I did not get from church or books or work at the
Firestone Store. He provided us passports to all kinds of things that would
otherwise have been unavailable. All of a sudden, as if in response to my
deepest needs, he appeared and took me to Los Angeles, to Hollywood,
and to Manhattan: in 1956, we were the first band from Mississippi and
possibly from the South to march in the Rose Bowl Parade in Pasadena,
maybe the first to play for crowds in the newly-opened Disneyland; in
1959 we marched in Macy's Thanksgiving Day Parade in New York City
and performed a trickstep routine for national television; on the way to
New York we stopped in Washington, D.C. long enough to tour and to
play a full concert in the brand-new Senate Office Building auditorium.
Later bands, after I had graduated, marched in parades and performed
in Atlanta and St. Louis, and at the Orange Bowl, the Gator Bowl, and
the Cotton Bowl. In New York Charlie made arrangements for some of
us older and cooler cats, even though underage, to have an evening at
Birdland—*Birdland!*—which disappeared some years later but which in
its time and for years was Mecca indeed for jazz aficionados, a paradise
to return to. No name band played the evening we were there, but Sarah
Vaughan was in the audience having a drink and, invited to take a bow,

she sang an impromptu set with the band—casual, at home, routine. Magic.

If I seem to romanticize these years, I can only plead guilty. I know no other way to give any sense of how extraordinary, how magical, they were, or what they meant to a small-city boy who got these chances by no particular effort of his own but purely by the luck of the school board's chance hiring of Charlie Newman: they could have hired any number of band directors who would have been content just to march at halftime of football games and to do well at State Band Contest every spring in Jackson. (We did our share of that sort of service, of course: we performed at football games, pep rallies, Christmas parades in Picayune and, for several years, at Mardi Gras in New Orleans, until it got too raucous to be worth the effort.) But they hired Charlie.

He was less a musician than a showman and he took great pride in the quality of the marching shows he put together. He insisted on operating at the cutting edge of band entertainment: the Picayune band, the "Pride of the Tung Belt," was among the first high school bands to use twirling bass drums for marching, for example; black lights for when we'd turn off the stadium lights during the halftime show for eerie illumination of the majorettes as they danced. At our and his best, we were most noted for really intricate "tricksteps," marching routines that were years ahead in intricacy and precision of what anybody else in the region was doing. In one routine, which Charlie called "Going Ape," the band divided itself in half, then into quarters, then eighths, and so on until each individual band member was an isolated unit marching in his or her own direction; then we reversed and reassembled. We did all this to the singular tapping of a snare drum, all the while engaging in a series of complicated movements with our feet, turns and feints with our bodies. I recently saw Charlie's film of this routine; it's still dazzling. When we performed it at State Band Contest, we got a standing ovation from the other bands, something then unheard of.

The band's success was not without controversy. Some years ago Charlie wrote and published a book of memoirs* about those years, both the public success and the less public, darker side of the success. The book is mostly about the band's trips and its successes but it is also, in its own way and completely incidentally, a fairly interesting social history of some of the internal dynamics of such small cities as Picayune. I experienced a good deal of the animosity toward the band that Charlie writes about, but I learned from his book several things that I did not know about the kinds of conflicts and oppositions in the town that the band's, and Charlie's, success seem to have occasioned.

As in all communities, band was an adjunct to football, a service organization whose function was to provide spectacle and noise during time-outs and other gaps in the action. If band members incidentally learned some music along the way, that was acceptable and even desirable, but mainly we existed to accompany: to play the national anthem before football games, to entertain the crowds at halftime while the football players took a breather, to provide fanfares for the homecoming queen and her court to take the field, to create various enthusiasms during the game, helping the cheerleaders by playing "Fight"—a raucous trumpet fanfare solo, thrilling but perilous because the final run ended on a high C and *everybody* listened to hear you either make or "bust" the final note—every time the boys on the field needed encouragement. This is of course the way it was everywhere else, and the way it should have been in Picayune.

But the band's success, its national exposure, occurred during years when the football team's fortunes were going decidedly in the other direction. My memory has always had it that the team didn't even

---

*Charles S. Newman, *I Had It All with the Pride: A History of the Picayune Memorial High School "Pride of the Tung Belt" Band 1954–1971* (Clinton, Mississippi: The One House Publishing Co., 1992).

score, much less win, during my four high school years, until the final
game of my senior year when the team scored one touchdown, to the
immense disappointment of those of us who had come to relish the sweet
perfection we were courting; we probably did win some games during
those years, or at least score occasionally, but it pleases me to remember
it in my own way. In any case, the team's dismal lack of success ran
a stark and humiliating counterpoint to the band's meteoric rise; local
jokes included not very subtle variations on the theme, "Well, at least
we will have the band to watch. . . ."

We band members had long been accustomed to snide looks from
athletes, which let us know what they thought about our musical position
on the masculinity scale; doubtless these assumptions were a residual
affect, on both sides, of attitudes developed during those grammar and
junior high school years when we would get teased for having to practice
the piano, when even we didn't want to practice anything but baseball.
But during these years we found ourselves collectively and individually
being blamed for the team's misfortunes. On one occasion a grim-faced
head coach, a skinny meanspirited snivelling little twirp of a man, the
architect of the team's misfortunes, stood in school assembly and publicly
blamed the team's problems on the "big, strapping band boys" who
were in the band and not on the football field, where they should be.
Were we men or mice? Coach wanted to know. They were losing and
it was *my* fault! We band members were at first stunned into silence
and then began to giggle until shortly we were howling with laughter
from where we sat together in the back of the auditorium; soon the
laughter spread to the rest of the auditorium, even to most of the football
players themselves, even those who doubtless believed we were sissies,
who knew how ludicrous the coach's accusation was. Charlie, who had
been listening from the back of the auditorium, began walking forward,
shouting for recognition from the principal, Mr. Slaughter. At the front,
Charlie confronted the coach—"Well, what do *you* think, Coach? Are

they men or mice? If they're mice, what good could they do your football team?"—and the entire student body lost it completely. Coach was not pleased to be laughed at. He stormed out of the auditorium and later brought pressure on the administration to have Charlie fired. Only years later did I understand how utterly unprofessional and inappropriate the coach's behavior was; but the era's assumptions about the importance of sports generally and football particularly was such that he thought he could get away with it.

Musicians have let athletes appropriate the high moral ground, especially in high school and college; we accede almost without challenge— no matter how it grates, we mostly bear it in silence—to the athletic establishment's publicity machines' constant hightoned selfserving claims that athletics are not just good but essential because they teach discipline and teamwork and that because they thrive on competition they are the best possible training ground for life: they build character because they teach people how to win and how to respond to defeat. These are, of course, claims as completely patronizing to and dismissive of other social activities as their operating assumptions about their moral grounding are presumptive—as though what musicians do, what band members do, does not require discipline or teamwork, and as though musical training, with its emphasis on harmony and cooperation rather than on competition, does not also "build character" and is not also a workable paradigm for social and political organization. At State Band Contest, for example, bands competed not against each other for a state championship but against a standard of musical and marching excellence that the judges held in their heads: theoretically, at any rate, every band that performed could get a Superior rating. Thus it is completely arguable that musical discipline, of whatever kind, is in fact a better training ground "for life" than athletics, where winning, being Number One, is more important than anything, and so is not even a reasonable preparation for life, much less the best one. A training ground for life?

I'd bet the house that, high athletic salaries notwithstanding, there are more people making more and better money in music than in athletics.

I—we—were of course of our own time and place and so were not able to understand this athletics-band competition so clearly as now I can, and in fact I felt something like a second-class citizen because I didn't play football. Football would certainly have been my father's preference for me, although he seemed in fact to have taken a good deal of pleasure, or at least interest, in my band activities: his support of my musical life may have been his finest hour.

At some deep level, I felt that I should have been playing football instead of the trumpet and was male enough actually to feel disappointed in myself and a disappointment to my father. I was sufficiently Baptist to be easily made to feel responsible for just about anything you'd accuse me of, so that the coach's accusations hit me with a peculiar nagging force that worked on me in a couple of ways. While one part of me knew that his was an outrageous complaint and that I had no desire whatever to play football, another part felt he was probably right: why *wasn't* I out there working for the greater glory? Why was I wasting all my vitality on something that weaklings and girls do? I felt slightly emasculate. In retrospect it is easy to see that one of the things Charlie—and other band directors—provided was a male model for those of us who just didn't want to play football, no matter what the pressures were. Even so, we band boys were sufficiently vulnerable to the charge of sissy to have established our own gender hierarchies, so that, for example, we considered as sissy and probably homosexual any male who became—in other bands; Charlie wouldn't have one—a drum *major*: this was clearly, to us, a woman's job.

So the coach's accusation was a kind of watershed for the big bad band boys, as we began to call ourselves—Larry Fletcher, Ronny Jones, Roland Travis, and James Whatley, among others—that gave us a kind of doubled and tripled ecstasy in our playing, from that moment on.

We who preferred sixteenth-note runs in the march trios to catching a touchdown pass, we who infinitely preferred grooving to "Shake Rattle & Roll" in the stands to blocking out a 250-pound tackle, had a mission. It was sweet, and got sweeter and sweeter on a finely honed edge that dripped with sarcasm, to sit in the stands and play more and more above ourselves in direct proportion to the team's—and especially the coach's—bottoming misfortunes. During those years we knocked ourselves out to provide better and better entertainment during the halftimes and to play louder and more wonderfully in the stands while the team was on the field: our little reminder to the coach, who we hoped not only heard every thrilling note but felt it too, as a concatenation of mosquitoes, say—and an occasional hornet. It was all perfectly legitimate: we were doing exactly what we were supposed to do. It was a particular pleasure to accompany the team to out-of-town games to perform; we were self-appointed avenging furies who were not, if we could help it, going to let him or the team escape us, ever.

More serious were events during the early years just after Charlie wangled the invitation from Pasadena and was trying to get local support for the band's trip to the Rose Bowl Parade. These events took place during years, as I recall, in which the football team was actually competitive, so that the animus against the band came from other elements in the community.

When Charlie proposed the California trip, in 1955, school administrators and civic leaders like Mayor Crosby immediately saw the possibilities in such a trip not just for the publicity it would bring to Picayune but also for the opportunities it would provide to enhance our educations, to "broaden our horizons." They jumped in enthusiastically to help us all raise an enormous amount of money—$20,000!—to help finance the venture. We needed about $150 per person, to be raised from fruitcake sales and other enterprises. Mr. Crosby all but guaranteed to donate from his own bottomless pocket whatever we couldn't raise. Pic

Moseley, the owner of Picayune's two movie theatres, told Charlie that the band would go to Pasadena even if he had to put folding chairs in his 18-wheeler and drive us there himself.

Other forces in Picayune were not so sanguine about such ventures into the outside world. Their opposition was xenophobic and racist: we might see black and white people together or get ideas about how other people lived, in that wild and crazy California, that could make us unhappy at home. I had no idea at the time how controversial the trip was or just how strongly opposed some elements of the town were; I was too busy selling fruitcakes. There were rumors that a gang of opponents was going to beat Charlie into submission, rumors sufficiently believable that the police provided him protection. They never attacked Charlie, but one night unknown assailants, probably football player/thugs and probably upon orders of the football coach (not our nemesis coach, who hadn't come to Picayune yet), attacked and hospitalized an older friend, Bobby Johnson. I knew about this attack: even I could see bandages. But I didn't know until years later, talking with Charlie about his book, that the attack had been anything but incidental, certainly not that it was motivated by the band's imminent trip out of town.

But cooler heads prevailed and we went. We boarded the train in Picayune, two special cars just for us, and rode for three days there and three days back. On the way home we stopped in El Paso and took a side trip into an actual foreign country—*Juarez*—and matched our bargaining talents with the local merchants. In California we marched in the Rose Bowl Parade on national television (and returned home to find out that a good deal of our moment of glory had been lost behind commercials for Minute Maid frozen orange juice); we played a concert in the pavilion at the just-opened Disneyland in Anaheim and for our concert got free admission to the park; we heard Dave Brubeck and Les Brown and His Band of Renown at the Hollywood Palladium; we ate at the Brown Derby; we hung around Hollywood and Vine; we saw black and white people together; we got ideas about how other people lived. Some of us believe we saw Marilyn Monroe shopping at the Farmer's Market.

i i .

Doing jazz had its drawbacks, all social. For a group of us jazz mostly estranged our ears from everything else. Jazz was "cool" and for listening we disdained the simplicity of rock and roll's monotonous one-key three-chord triplet rhythms in favor of the more complicated driving rhythms and structures of contemporary jazz. Kenton and others had begun experimenting with very complex African and Cuban rhythms. Rock and roll's piano, electric guitar, and occasional baritone sax seemed a thin and watery diet compared to the rich, multivoiced sonorities of the big band.

I had grown up listening to traditional, "classic" country music on Nashville radio and then on Picayune's WRJW, which began broadcasting in 1947, loving such Grand Old Opry voices as Hank Williams, especially Hank, Red Foley, Ernest Tubb, Little Jimmy Dickens—what a name!—, the funny boys Lonzo and Oscar, and all the others. B. J. Johnson was the disk jockey for WRJW and he himself played guitar and sang in his own country music band and had something of a local following; I never heard him live, since so far as I knew he and his band played mostly across the county and state lines at dance halls and juke joints that served alcoholic beverages, and so they got associated with places that I was not supposed to go. I have since learned how essential to the experience of traditional country music a dark room, a corner table, and a longneck beer are; they make the band not quite irrelevant, but simply one element in a total ambience wherein a really bad amateur band with lots of feeling can sometimes be more satisfying than a polished professional one.

I listened to country music almost exclusively until the rock-and-roll revolution in the mid-fifties, just about the time that fabulous diva Patsy Cline got started. I got cultured with my peers and then had time only for New Orleans's great WNOE, a rock-and-roll powerhouse of the fifties and sixties. But rock and roll lasted, for me, only a couple of years, until I met Charlie and became consumed with jazz. Though I continued to listen to rock, I did it on the sly, since I had to have the radio on, and rock came in to Picayune from everywhere; but with few exceptions—Elvis; anybody remember Tommy Sands?—it became less and less interesting to me. My memories of rock and roll are now mostly manufactured from "Greatest Hits Of" collections, which remind me of what I then listened to on the radio without making a connection between what I heard and the name of the artist. I spent more and more time listening to New Orleans's WWL radio, especially in the late evening, when Dick Martin and his "Night Flight" show broadcast the best jazz going, big band and combo. Martin chatted by phone regularly with Stan Kenton, the Four Freshmen, and others whose music I adored. In effect, I missed the burgeoning country music scene of the fifties, the sort of high point of "traditional" country music, and neglected most of rock and roll as it developed because of my shifting allegiances and apparent inability to embrace more than one kind of music at a time. I had not yet listened to Beethoven, except as the theme music to the *Huntley-Brinkley Report* on NBC. Mozart? Opera? Hush.

There was little if any local resistance to rock and roll in Picayune; resistance was never serious enough to ally us with the moralistic condemnation of rock that we read about in the paper and saw on television; certainly there was no resistance of the sort we saw in that whole series of movies during the fifties that pitted teenagers and rock against stodgy arrhythmical bluenoses who finally succumbed to rock's rhythms and enthusiasm. My father quite liked it; he took some pride in the fact that Elvis was a Mississippi boy, and shared with me jokes about the Elvis phenomenon (one about Elvis the Pelvis and his brother Enos, which he thought was hilarious). He liked Fats Domino and Little Richard, The Coasters, The Platters, though he mostly preferred Nat King Cole and would watch Cole's television show with great pleasure, except when Cole would embrace or otherwise touch white guests when he introduced them.

One of the things that problematized rock and roll for me was that I didn't dance. Baptists frowned upon dancing and so naturally I took the pledge one fervent night at a revival, when the evangelist asked those who would vow not to dance to come to the front. What could I do? I was by no means the only person in Picayune to have taken that pledge, but I certainly was the only one to stick by it: I was a person of principle in those days and principle was then, and it continues to be, frequently useful. In spite of my mastery of Charlie's intricate trick-step routines in the marching band I was, on the dance floor, klutzy and selfconscious and not a very good dancer anyway, so the chance to opt out on principle was one I was happy to exercise. Jazz offered me a sort of safe haven to retreat into, though that too got complicated by my Baptist upbringing.

Jazz took me mostly out of rock-and-roll culture through a virulent sort of amateur *snobisme* that made it possible for me to be more sophisticated than my non-jazz friends. During my senior year I brought this snobbishness to a peak when I, by all but begging, inherited a half hour radio show on WRJW; the station devoted that half-hour every Wednesday afternoon to activities at Picayune High; the show was hosted by a high school disc jockey, who was to play some records and to interview students and faculty. My predecessor's music of choice had been rock and roll and some country. I hit the airwaves with Kenton, Frank Sinatra, and Dizzy Gillespie! I had actual visions that somehow I was going to change the listening habits of people whose preferred musical tastes were Hank Williams and Little Jimmy Dickens. I think the station manager was glad when my year was up; I know B. J. was.

For a couple of years, when I was in the eighth and ninth grades, Charlie organized a group of us into our own jazz band—a "big" band, as we say, of nearly twenty people—a group handpicked from the cooler cats in the marching band. Two incredible side men—Larry Fletcher, a cornet player, and Jo Lon Easton, who played baritone sax—formed the jazz nucleus of our group; they could play the solo "rides" above our rhythmic riffs and fugues. From where I sat as the fourth-chair trumpet, this too was magic. Charlie was ambitious; we practiced classic Glenn Miller, Woody Herman, and Stan Kenton "charts" for hours but essentially had nowhere to perform them publicly. I believe we played for a couple of high school assemblies but I can't recall any other performances, until one year Charlie volunteered us to provide music for the high school dances—a decision that led directly to the band's dissolution, because many members of the band, those less devoted to jazz than the faithful handful of us, preferred to dance at the prom rather than provide music for others to dance to.

I, of course, who didn't dance on principle, made the band's—my— playing at dances into a moral crisis about which I consulted my Baptist conscience, resident in the First Baptist pastor's office. It told me what I knew he would: if it was wrong for me to dance, how could it be right for me to play for others to? Fortunately, I was yet again let off the hook of choice, of confronting Charlie with my crisis; by the time my conscience got the better of me, the dancers had already managed to break up the orchestra, and I never had to resign. My life is, indeed, a series of moral choices I didn't have to make.

iii.

Mississippi was certainly, in most important ways, the "closed society" that James Silver called it and that the Hederman brothers and the White Citizens' Council worked overtime to preserve and protect. But it was not completely closed, ever; not even the Hedermans could keep the rest of the world completely out. Nor was Mississippi ever the cultural wasteland, the "Sahara of the Bozart" that H. L. Mencken called the entire South and that many folks continue to believe that everything southern except Atlanta still is. There were lots of leaks, lots of reciprocities with the rest of the world that worked to make Mississippi the wildly paradoxical state it is.

The easiest thing would be to print even a short version of the dazzling list of writers that everybody in the civilized world has heard of, but that might be a gratuitous insult to other states and many countries and, besides, there's hardly enough room here.* Suffice it to name musicians ranging from Leontyne Price and Milton Babbitt to B. B. King, Tammy Wynette, Charlie Pride, and, of course, Elvis; Turner Catledge was editor of the *New York Times* during the volatile civil rights years; Nash K. Burger edited *The New York Times Book Review* for many years beginning in the mid-forties; Jefferson biographer Dumas Malone and his brother Kemp, one of the most important philologists of the twentieth century; painters Walter Anderson and Theora Hamblett and William Dunlap; potters and sculptors George Ohr and Lee and Pup McCarty; novelist Gloria Norris was for two years editor-in-chief of the Book of the Month Club. Oprah Winfrey is a successful escapee

---

*OK. Here are some I can think of without even trying, and not in any particular order: Faulkner, Welty, Richard Wright, Barry Hannah, Ellen Douglas, Richard Ford, Tennessee Williams, Walker Percy, Margaret Walker Alexander, Stark Young, James Street, Jim Seay, Elizabeth Spencer, Hodding Carter, Gloria Norris, Shelby Foote, Charles G. Bell, William Alexander Percy, Willie Morris, Jack Butler, Henry Bellamann, Joan Williams, Thomas Hal Phillips, Evans Harrington, John Grisham, Larry Brown. *Lives of Mississippi Authors, 1817–1967*, ed. James B. Lloyd (Jackson: University Press of Mississippi, 1981) devotes nearly 500 double-columned pages to biographical sketches of just some of the Mississippians who had published at least one book up to 1967. I'd bet it would take nearly that many more pages to list the ones since 1967.

from the state, as is Morgan Freeman, and Mississippians have starring roles in *Northern Exposure* and *Sisters*; *Major Dad*'s Gerald McRaney was a skinny fourth-grader in Picayune who sometimes hung around our house to play with my younger brother. These are all, of course, escapees: but they had to learn somewhere that there was both something to escape from and something to escape to. In addition, Mississippi boasts numerous pockets of concentrated culture—in Jackson, Tupelo, Greenville, Greenwood, Laurel, Oxford, for example; artist colonies at Alison's Wells in the thirties and forties—as well as a dense scattering throughout the state of very sophisticated people.

But such lists of extraordinary people don't tell the entire story of Mississippi's rapprochement with the *haute culture* of the outside world. People have for generations made it to Memphis, Chicago, or New York for theatre and music, and to New Orleans, where on separate occasions I heard the New Orleans Symphony perform Beethoven's Ninth Symphony and then Elisabeth Schwarzkopf sing Strauss's *Four Last Songs*. But for as long as I've known anything about it, Jackson, Meridian, Tupelo, and the Gulf Coast have maintained symphony orchestras; these and other towns have opera seasons (even if the season consists only of one or two productions), support travelling subscription concert series and little theatres; Hattiesburg has a very active theatre season, and relies on the University of Southern Mississippi symphony orchestra for its music; Itzhak Perlman recently performed as guest artist with the very fine USM Symphony. Several cities, especially Jackson and those near universities, regularly host a variety of chamber and solo concerts. One of the South's, maybe one of the nation's, most ambitious and successful professional theatre companies is Jackson's New Stage, founded in 1964, in the midst of the civil rights crisis. New Stage opened its first season with a powerful production of *Who's Afraid of Virginia Woolf?*, using all local talent; I was a charter subscriber to its first season. For years now Jackson has been one of five permanent rotating host cities sponsoring the International Ballet Competition, along with Moscow, Paris, Helsinki, and Varna, Bulgaria. The Mississippi Institute of Arts and Letters, founded in 1978, gives annual awards of $1,000 each to Mississippi writers, artists, photographers, and composers, for outstanding work done in the previous year; the institute has never wanted for outstanding candidates in any category.

I don't indulge in these lists as a matter of competition with other states or countries, no matter what I wrote earlier, but rather as a matter of simple astonishment at what is after all not a bad record for a backward state. If the quality of the performances or of the artists might cause New Yorkers or Clevelanders to sneer or (more politely) roll their eyes; if one Jackson audience in the sixties gave a standing ovation to Mantovani; and if literally hundreds of Mississippi artists are frequently given to painting magnolias on a black background, it is still an utterly astonishing thing to consider the sheer quantity of artistic and cultural activity in Mississippi, almost from its beginnings. How could a state with so little do so much, create the climate for such a wide range of cultural activity, not to say world-class achievement? Do not tell me, as some have tried to do, that the amount and quality of "culture" in Mississippi are a direct reaction against the state's poverty and backwardness: if that were the case, why have Arkansas, Georgia, and Alabama not produced their own equivalents?

Thus culture, artistic nourishment, has always been available in Mississippi to such folks as wanted it and had the leisure and desire to find it. Picayune was not such a cultural "pocket" in Mississippi, and I was by no means aware of what was happening in the rest of the state. We read no Faulkner or Welty at Picayune High School, and I do not remember ever hearing those names breathed aloud in Picayune, not even by folks who might have known what kinds of image problems

Faulkner, at least, was causing Mississippi during the mid-fifties by his outspoken comments on the racial issue. From my high school reading lists or discussions about literature, I could have gotten no proof that anybody had written anything after 1850, much less anybody in the twentieth century, *much less* anybody in Mississippi.

Even so, Picayune was not without its cultural and artistic resources, in both the general and specific senses: Mrs. Trula Seal was one of several women who painted, the driving force in a ladies' painting society. Mrs. Yett owned and occasionally played for us, at her home and in school assemblies, a *cello*, a curious gorgeous wondrous highbrow instrument; on two or three occasions the Jackson Youth Symphony toured the state, stopping to give concerts in such places as Picayune, bringing with them kids our own ages who played cellos and violins and violas as though to do so were the most natural, the least amazing, thing in the world. By the late fifties and the early sixties, doubtless thanks to the influx of folks to work at NASA, Picayune too had a subscription concert series, and I came home on more than one occasion to hear the New Orleans Symphony perform in the brand-new high school auditorium.

In all kinds of ways we were virtually under siege by the outside world. Even with all the Hedermans' many fingers in the leaking dike, Mississippi couldn't keep the entire world at bay. My family had one of the first televisions in Picayune, I believe, bought in late 1949; we watched a celebration—I think it was in Times Square, but it could have been something in New Orleans—that very New Year's Eve. It was a 12½-inch screen—the cutting edge of technology—and by the mid- to late-fifties we kids had access to the Crosbys' color RCA: *Bonanza* was glorious!

From WDSU-NBC in New Orleans, that little television channelled the rest of the world in to my living room, in a gullywasher of news. The information highway was then barely a footpath in the wilderness, but the world sluiced in to my life through that square foot of electronics just as, only a few years later, its cousins would bring Mississippi's and Alabama's and Arkansas's turmoil into the living rooms of the rest of the world. On good days, if the weather were mostly clear and the wind had not turned the antenna a bit, we got excellent reception: cool, clear, magical black and white. Of an evening I would stare endlessly and impatiently at the test pattern while waiting for the evening broadcasts to begin, around 6 p.m., then watched Kukla, Fran, and Ollie, Pinkie Lee, Howdy Doody, and Hopalong Cassidy, and the news, always the news: Huntley and Brinkley, Dave Garroway and J. Fred Muggs, and, when WWL began broadcasting in late 1957, Edward R. Murrow and Walter Cronkite. More to the point for my purposes here, though, is that that little television brought Toscanini and the New York Philharmonic into my living room, the Hallmark Hall of Fame and Omnibus brought fabulous drama. Leonard Bernstein's Young People Concerts were a gift from the gods, a revelation: not his words so much as the sound of that orchestra, even from our television's single speaker. I wasn't in a position to understand much of what Bernstein said; I was too busy absorbing the music to pay any attention to his words, not knowing then that music needed to be explained, or could be.

So it is not literally true that I had not heard Beethoven by the time I discovered jazz in 1956; I had, but I had had no real context for it until Charlie Newman provided it for me. My initial nourishment on big band jazz has left me with a completely inarticulate and almost totally uncritical pleasure in the massive clashing and clanging of Beethoven, Mahler, the operas of Wagner and Strauss and Verdi, even the more preposterously grandiose and swaggering parts of Puccini's *Turandot*. I have only in the past several years come to appreciate the more subtle and intricate accomplishments of chamber music and of small jazz combos. And though if I have a second life I'd like to return as a jazz flutist or a bull bass fiddle player in a jazz quartet, for the most part it's still, for me, the bigger and louder the better.

iv.

In 1933 Faulkner wrote an essay in which he argued that art in the South was different from art in the North. In the North art is a routine part of everyday life: the factory worker goes home after work, has a beer and dinner, then goes as a matter of course to do his turn taking up tickets at the local opera house or theatre. In the South, Faulkner claims, art is something apart from the quotidian; it has to define itself as spectacle in order to exist at all. I know whereof he speaks but I think he was only partly right, and the differences he describes may have more to do with large cities and small towns than with region. Many folks in Picayune would not have cared to sit still for a symphony concert, certainly not for a cello sonata or an opera; all of these would have provided spectacle, but of an alien sort which would therefore be an interruption, a diversion from the ordinary movements of their daily lives. Most got their aesthetic nourishment, whatever it was, from television, which they could watch out of the corner of their eyes while reading the newspaper or shelling peas or shining shoes or clipping their toenails. Classical music's sheen of primness, of limp-wristedness, its associations with the formal stuffiness of people in tuxedos or of tenors and sopranos with purple faces singing in languages they didn't know, made too-formidable claims on their energies and their capacities not at all in intelligence or feeling but in training and exposure, or perhaps simply in the time available to them to learn something new. With so many demands and pressures on them every day, how expect them to work so hard to break their old habits of relaxation?

Church music was an agreeable exception for everybody. The First Baptist Church boasted a fairly large choir. Picayune would crowd into the auditorium when at Christmas and Easter we performed the appropriate portions of Handel's *Messiah*, especially if we hired professional musicians from New Orleans to accompany us and singers from the

New Orleans Seminary to do the solos. The congregation faithfully and enthusiastically stood during the "Hallelujah Chorus," knowing that tradition required us to, and cooed appropriately at the performance's conclusion. I mean no irony or condescension or criticism in recalling this; a good deal of the warmth in my recollections of Picayune resides in First Baptist's music program. Our responses to *Messiah* were genuine; our amateur performances moved us deeply. I know that there were many people in Picayune sophisticated enough to know the difference between a good performance and a bad one, but I do suspect that in truth most members of the First Baptist Church preferred the sweeter, simpler melodies and harmonies of a John W. Peterson cantata and that they looked forward to hearing our singing sisters, Jo Ann Newman and Audie Smith, Charlie's wife and sister-in-law, sing their lovely duet, "Out of the Ivory Palaces," or to be joined by the church's music director, Paul Padgett, in a trio.

What made *Messiah* a treat were its familiarity, its unarguable status as "classical" music, its English language, our sense of cultural sophistication in hearing or performing it or even knowing when to stand, and, perhaps most centrally, its religious message: its elegant combination of aesthetics and utility. Combined with the orchestra from New Orleans, *Messiah* easily qualified as spectacle; we could relax into an aesthetic experience, no matter how good or bad the performance was. *Messiah's* religious content gave culture a function other than pleasure, and so made it acceptable.

I suspect that band succeeded for many of the same reasons, but mostly in the band's combination of spectacle with utility too, the band's willingness to function as part of the support systems for more familiar and acceptable forms of leisure activity, like football and Christmas parades, without calling on anybody to think of beauty. It was all the better if we played familiar music—those arrangements of "Shake Rattle and Roll" or other contemporary popular songs, or old Sousa standards like "National Emblem," the trio of which was as familiar and friendly (we could sing along: "Oh, the monkey wrapped his tail around the flagpole, showed his asshole . . .") as the fanfare finale of the *William Tell Overture*, which we heard every week on television. I suspect that Picayune tolerated our formal band concerts, or at least accepted them, even graciously, once a year, as part of the price they had to pay for a loud marching group that could perform at football games and in local parades; if we learned some music, if the band gave Picayune national exposure, that was gravy—so long as we showed up every Friday night at the football game.

A good deal of a band's function is to recreate the circus, to invoke the carnival atmosphere of celebration and ecstasy, of the escape from the daily; spectacle is a central part of carnival. But small towns fear carnival's looseness, its untidiness, its potential for a problematical pleasure, and so perhaps the band also simultaneously provides an acceptable way of having carnival and of controlling it too, of keeping it in bounds, as spectacle, as something we watch from a distance: the color, the sensuous brassy outrageous and familiar music, the multicolored flags and uniforms, the majorettes—our daughters and sisters or those of our friends—to ogle respectfully and respectably.

I gather that the history of high school bands has yet to be written—the phenomenon, I mean. I'd be interested to know when band became part of the high school and junior high school curricula, when the small bands of adult musicians, who played of an evening in the bandstand in the park on the Fourth of July or Armistice Day, or upon civic occasions, were replaced by the high school marching band, and when band got appropriated by football. I have tried without success to interest a foreign filmmaker in doing a documentary on the cultural phenomenon of the spectacle surrounding football—the cheerleaders, the majorettes, baton twirlers, the flagbearers, the band's formation of school letters and logos on the field during halftime, all driven by brassily diverting fanfares and marches. This is a uniquely American activity that most Americans simply take for granted; but I'll bet that other countries would be astonished, anthropologically speaking, to understand what we do.

v.

Thanks to *Picayune Item* editor Chance Cole, Charlie's bands and Picayune had great rapport over the years; Cole constantly touted the band and its accomplishments. When Cole died, Charlie has told me, something went out of that rapport and out of Charlie. About the same time Charlie left Picayune for another town, long after I had become a professor in Texas, Picayune's popular and successful basketball coach also left to take another job. Coach Ladner had taken the team from obscurity to state-wide recognition as a basketball powerhouse. Picayune virtually prostrated itself with grief over his departure, showered him with fetes and gifts and good wishes, all of which he deserved, for he was indeed a nice person and had done much for the dozens and dozens of kids he had coached in the few years he was in Picayune. Charlie left Picayune without any public fanfare or even notice. As far as I know, the only public goodbye he got, the only public thanks for an important job well done, was the letter I wrote to the *Item* in behalf of the hundreds and hundreds of Picayune High students to whom, over a period of nearly two decades, he had given the inestimable gift not just of music but of possibility, perhaps the best gift of all.

Class and Manners

Almost from the beginning of the Firestone Store's existence until the end of my freshman summer in college, I worked with and for my father on Saturdays and during summers. I have only recently come to appreciate what a useful and interesting vantage that perch provided me for meeting a wide and representative variety of people: blacks and whites of the lowest economic rungs, whom I waited on when they came into the store as customers, whose tires I changed while they watched and passed the time talking with me, and into and on top of and under whose homes I went climbed and crawled when collecting overdue bills, when delivering and installing merchandise, and when, all too frequently, repossessing that merchandise after they had failed to pay on the schedule promised. I knew white middle- and upper-class folks, in so far as Picayune had an "upper" class, all things being relative; city and county officials and politicians—supervisors, sheriffs, deputies, city managers; local media folks from the *Picayune Item* and country music radio station WRJW; Firestone representatives and sales people from offices in New Orleans and Akron, Ohio; lawyers and other folks in various businesses around the city. I was also frequently sent on errands—to pick up merchandise that we didn't keep in stock, usually: a tire of a size that we didn't keep or had sold out of, for example—to larger Firestone dealerships in Bogalusa, Louisiana, in Hattiesburg, and frequently to Firestone's and Philco's regional distribution offices in New Orleans.

Since there was but one school system—for whites, I mean—, one junior high and one high school, I had friends whose parents and grandparents were part of Picayune's older if not completely "upper" crust. Through junior high, my best friend was Osmond Crosby III, son of L. O. Crosby Jr., the closest thing to a patriarch Picayune had: he at least owned the largest number of jobs in the area, had the largest payroll, and was, with his brothers and father (whom I never met), the richest man in town. Through Oz, I got to hang around with him on occasion. My membership at the First Baptist Church brought me in contact with various other people who were part of Picayune's history, like Barney Whitfield, whom I knew only as a kindly old man, an insurance salesman, and his wife, Mrs. Barney. I didn't learn until much later, reading some county and local histories, that Barney was among the town's earliest citizens, and so worth knowing if I had grown up with any sense of history. But it never occurred to me that any of these folks might have pasts, either in or out of Picayune, since I didn't have one yet. I didn't find out until several years after he had died that others in Picayune did think about history: Grady Thigpen Sr., known widely as "Grampaw Grady," another pioneer in the area and a coeval of Barney's, was writing a series of books about Pearl River County and south Mississippi history based on his own recollections as a young man and on his interviews with folks even older and more pioneering than he. Thus the peculiar circumstances of my position growing up in Picayune gave me access to a wide variety of people, to a variety of visions, to a variety of relationships with Picayune's past and present. I would have seen more, I guess, if I had known that there was more to look at. But I was not aware until recently of how little, or how much either, I did see.

With its population of 6,707, Picayune was slightly more than one third the size Faulkner claimed for Jefferson on the map he drew to accompany *Absalom, Absalom!* in 1936. But he, or his narrators, always treated Jefferson as a small town of the southern tradition, in which unmistakable class divisions separated aristocratic blueblooded old families from wealthy plantation owners from nouveaux riches from bourgeois merchant from day laborer from white trash from Negro; as a small stiflingly intimate community in which everybody knew everybody else's business and from whose collective bluenose nobody could ever really escape. Yet even though Picayune had roughly one third Jefferson's population (a bit larger total population, blacks and whites, than Jefferson's 6,298 white inhabitants), and even with my own various tendrils into disparate elements of the community, I had absolutely no sense that I knew everybody in Picayune, much less that I knew, or had any access to, their "business." To be sure, I doubtless missed a lot because of my tender years and excessive naïveté, but I was no less sensitive to rumor, gossip, and scandal than anybody else, and kept at least one ear open wide. One night Karen Whitecloud's aunt, who lived with the Whiteclouds just up the street from me, committed suicide, the only suicide I remember during my time in Picayune. I believe to this day that I heard the shot, the loneliest sound I have ever heard. But I remember nothing of scandal or gossip to explain why she did it. We were respectfully content to let the Whiteclouds bear their grief in silence.

There were class divisions and consciousness in Picayune, of course, else it would not have occurred to my father to worry that I might be seen walking home one afternoon. But class divisions were not at all clearly defined. Indeed, they were fluid and shifting, moving along a variety of constantly intersecting lines, and shaping themselves around a number of social, financial, and religious centers. There were really no "old" families, no proud ancestors for late-arrivers to be awed into submission by, to be "accepted" or "rejected" by, no old money that already had the town's economy completely sewed up, since, as I say, there was no real town or substantial money either until well after the turn of the century and since so many of the town's "founders" and developers—Crosby, Eastman Tate, S. G. Thigpen, Barney Whitfield, Claiborne McDonald—lived well into my own lifetime, and were still in the process of making whatever money there was to be made. Doubtless they will be "old families" very soon, if they are not already, as Picayune reaches its centennial.

In any case, if there were class problematics in Picayune, I had no sense of them, and here I again make my standard disclaimer, about the real possibility that I missed seeing things right in front of my eyes. How others felt, I do not know, but I was not jealous of my friend Osmond's affluence, partly because I knew that his father and grandfather had worked to make their money, but mostly because the Crosbys seemed essentially indifferent to the distinctions that money creates. They seemed much more interested in its usefulness than in whatever of prestige or power it bestowed or the self-adornment and -indulgence it allowed; I grant that it is easier to be indifferent to something you have lots of than to something you desperately need. But the Crosbys constantly funnelled money back into the community in the form of donations to the YMCA, for example; they helped build a new hospital and library in Picayune and the chapel at the First Baptist Church; they made huge contributions to the creation of Boy Scout Camp Ti'ak, just north of Picayune at Wiggins, and made large contributions to our band's trips to California and New York. These were just the donations I knew about, the public ones; I have no doubt there were others. Mr. Crosby went along with us on the train to California as a chaperon and he was in all kinds of ways one of us boys, without airs or pretensions, mansion and large grounds notwithstanding; he frequently came to our Scout campouts and seemed to enjoy walking with us through the woods; every summer on Oz's birthday he drove a carload of us to New Orleans to treat us to a day at Pontchartrain Beach Amusement Park because, he made it clear by his actions, he enjoyed being with us. He did not drive a new car every year or dress as though he ever gave a thought to anything more demanding than comfort. When we got old enough to drive, Oz drove not a snappy new roadster every year, which the Crosbys could well have afforded, but a '53 Chevy. Some others, without Mr. Crosby's money, always seemed far more pretentious, far more concerned with appearances and with status, than he ever did. Mrs. Crosby always took her part with other mothers in school projects, class picnics, and the life of the community.

There was other money in Picayune, but if it reached Crosby amounts I do not know it. Doctors seemed to do very well, especially after the construction of Crosby Memorial Hospital made Picayune a regional medical center, and there must have been a legal community, but I can only remember two or three lawyers—blind Ray Merle Stewart, "Little" Grady Thigpen, and Delos Burkes, our representative in the state legislature—and I do not know how affluent they were as a group. Of bankers there were two: Pete Cooper, president of the First National Bank, and L. D. Megehee, who retired as superintendent of Picayune schools in order to become president of the older Bank of Picayune. Most of the other, the non-Crosby, money in Picayune was held sort of collectively by merchants such as Grampaw Grady Thigpen, whose Thigpen Hardware was an amoeba-like enterprise that dealt in home and construction supplies, lumber, home appliances, fishing and hunting gear; Hal Schrock's Western Auto Store; Bill Alexander's oil and gas enterprises; R. J. Williams's various enterprises; Claiborne McDonald's funeral home; Hooker Quick's and Buzzy Grice's hardware, building, and construction store; Thurston Wilkes's Oldsmobile-Cadillac, Jack Pearson's Ford, and R.D. Stockstill's Chrysler-Plymouth dealership; J.E. Mitchell's Department Store and Jacob "Jakie" Carp's Boston Store. None of these, as I gathered, had money in Crosby amounts, but they all lived what seemed to me lives of relative affluence. My father was on his way to his own place among these folks when he died in 1968.

I suspect that the most significant class divisions in Picayune, aside from the paramount one of race, were those between city and country folks: those seem to have been the crucial elements for my father, at any rate. Doubtless others, like my father, had grown up in the country, had moved to the city for its amenities and its greater economic opportunities, and also, like him, had retained just enough of their roots in the rural to still feel a countryman's sense of being somehow out of place in the city—perhaps socially awkward or, more likely, socially in arrears. I don't know how keenly my father felt the difference between himself and those from rural origins similar to his own who had come to the city and made it. I do know that he sometimes felt rather sharply the differences between his rural education and background and that of those from more urban backgrounds. He was a little intimidated by what he would have assumed to be the greater sophistication of those with more education and wider experience than he, though he would not have used the word "sophistication" in any way that would have assumed his own inferiority.

At the same time, he very much enjoyed associating with more polished folks, enjoyed being their equals, in Rotary Club and church and other civic organizations. He described to me a moment one evening at such a meeting, when the master of ceremonies asked each person to stand and introduce himself or herself to the group. He said that he began to feel uncomfortable, somewhat out of place among these folks, and that he fretted a bit as the others described their backgrounds and their college degrees. But by the time his turn came he had convinced himself that he needn't be ashamed of his background, that he should rather be proud that even without a college education he had made of himself a person worthy to be hanging out with such people. When his turn came he simply said that he had been educated in the Monticello, Mississippi, School System. The telling points in his story are his moment of fretting and his need to convince himself that he was worthy to be among such people—the *bump* that made accepting himself and his rural background a conscious and deliberate act, an act of will. This, too, is an episode in our relationship that has curiously stuck with me over the years. I have wondered why he told me this story in such detail. To let me know what he had overcome in order to get where he had gotten? To make me proud of him? To make me proud of me?

The next most significant class division was, I think, that between employer and employee—the late-proletarian bourgeoisie-wannabe and the current proletarian—but that perhaps only to the extent that the employer had significantly more disposable money than the employee: that is, to the extent that his assets were not completely tied up in the business itself, as ours were in the Firestone Store, so that the distance between Grampaw Grady or Hooker Quick and the lowliest of their numerous employees, or that between L. O. Crosby and the lowliest of his, was much greater than that between my father and any of his employees, who excluding me and my brother never numbered more than three at any time: a sales clerk, a bookkeeper/office manager, a boy to install the tires, repair lawn mowers and appliances, and make deliveries. But even so, many employees, especially some of the older ones, were, given the nature of the business, likely to have been coeval in the business with the founder in all but the financial investment, to have helped build the business to its present state. As with the Firestone Store, owner and employee would have worked together and/or interchangeably on any and all of the business's functions—indeed, my father died from the overexertion of changing a truck tire, the hardest and most menial of the store's jobs—so that there could easily have been unrestricted social intercourse, even close friendship, between employer and employee. On numerous occasions over the years my father employed my uncles and cousins to work with and for him, and during the late forties my family did a good deal of socializing with the Schrock family, when my father worked for Western Auto. Finally, employer and employee in Picayune might well share a pew or be deacons in the same church or have children or grandchildren in the band or on the cheerleader squad or football team or in the same class at school; perhaps their children dated each other or were otherwise involved in close friendships. There was too much commonality, too many specific sites for coming together, for class divisions, as usually understood, to be too severe.

Perhaps the most interesting division was between those who drank alcohol—at least of the cocktail variety—and those who didn't. I can't claim, of course, to know everybody who did and who didn't drink. Pearl River County was a very dry county during my life there; drinkers bought their liquor in New Orleans or on the Gulf Coast or just across the Hancock County line and drank at home rather than in local restaurants or bars. I suspect that there was a lot more imbibing in Picayune than I had any reason to know about, though I knew only of one person who was well known to be an alcoholic. My parents didn't drink, but that, my father claimed, was not at all because he disapproved or thought it immoral (though given his Baptist background he had every reason to think it an evil thing), but rather because some of his uncles and cousins were alcoholics and he was afraid he might like the taste too much himself. I of course disapproved completely of alcohol in all forms, clucked disapprovingly and shook my head at my friends' reports of their various encounters with the demon rum or the demon vodka or the demon beer. Even so, I associated drinking among whites with a kind of sophistication that did not come from Picayune, with people who came from or had had a good deal of contact with the world outside Picayune: the more highly educated white-collar folks who came to work for Crosby Chemicals, say, or doctors and lawyers. Of course our ears, our paper, and our lore were filled with stories of Negro drinking, Negro fights, at such black establishments as the Blue Goose Cafe.

Baptists who drank at cocktail parties seem to have done so at their own peril, always with an eye to a vigilante community. I once walked in on an older friend from First Baptist chugging a highball one afternoon with the parents of a friend I was visiting. I noted it but didn't think much about it until a couple of days later when my father mentioned to me that this person, an acquaintance at church and at Rotary but not one with whom my parents otherwise socialized, had called him to apologize if he had in any way offended me. "He doesn't believe there's anything wrong with a little drink now and then," my father explained, "but he was upset to think he might have set you a bad example." I thought this odd. He may truly have been tender of my sensibilities because I was by that time a ministerial aspirant, but I rather suspect that something in his own Baptist soul figured he had gotten caught, somehow, and in calling my father instead of me he was claiming a vague sort of class or age solidarity with him that would absolve him of wrongdoing. An aspiring preacher, I seemed already to have assumed, willy-nilly, the mantle of public disapprobation that communities force ministers to wear, and which would eventually be among the things forcing, or allowing, me to abandon the ministry for more secular pursuits: as a teenager I could not go into the barber shop without a noticeable alteration in the air and demeanor of barbers and customers.

One prominent family, members at First Baptist, faced a moral crisis when planning their daughter's wedding. Our pastor once told me that he and the family had spent much time together considering whether they should serve champagne at the reception. They did. The pastor assisted at the wedding in the church but didn't attend the reception at their home: not so much in protest or condemnation, I suspect—he had already made his position on the subject clear—as simply not to be associated with it. I'm sure that was fine with the family and with all the other Baptists who attended the reception; had the pastor been there, champagne consumption would have sagged considerably and everybody, including the pastor, knew it. The primary problem would have been simple exposure: most Baptists feared the condemnation that the pastor symbolized more than they feared the pastor's particular disapproval. I grew up not drinking; and though I've made up for lost time since graduate school, I still never drink any kind of alcohol without at some level having to get past a moral *bump* of my own, the Baptist one that ingrained in me a real sense that alcohol is morally wrong.

The drinkers *tended* to be Presbyterians and Episcopalians; Baptists and Methodists mostly didn't, at least in theory: as I say, the lines were fluid. Generally speaking, Presbyterians and Episcopalians were white-collar types—doctors and lawyers and others of the few professional types, many of whom worked for Crosby Forest Products or Crosby Chemicals in one scientific or administrative capacity or another. Baptists and Methodists were generally blue-collar, or at any rate from blue-collar and rural stock who even if they had made a lot of money were wont to stick to the old-time values of their raising, or at least the show of them.

There was a *very* small congregation of Christian Scientists, who had come to Picayune with Lamont Rowlands and established the church, in the block on the boulevard next to the First Baptist Church, in the late twenties; I didn't know any of them either. A Catholic church sat in a big lot near the high school—a sinister location, because the Catholics were out to recruit our young people, said the First Baptist pastor, as if Baptists weren't out to recruit the young Catholics. There was one prominent Jewish family in Picayune, Mr. and Mrs. Jacob Carp, their son Leonard and his wife Pauline, who ran The Boston Store, a clothing store, and from whom my father rented the Firestone Store building. So far as I knew, the Carps socialized and worshiped mostly in New Orleans.

ii.

In significant ways, class and social distinctions clung to age and gender and, of course, race, more than to money, at least in Picayune, though clearly money was a factor, as it always is everywhere, in every consideration. But age and gender and race always overrode money as the overt consideration in one-on-one, face-to-face encounters at any level, so that a wealthy white man might readily hold the door or give up a seat to an older black man or woman. Picayune's class structure, then, bore intimate relationships with its etiquettes, its manners. In what follows, I'm primarily concerned with relationships among white people, since I've already tried to comment on the complexities of interracial etiquette; much of what I say here applies to race, but it's much more complex, obviously, when race is a factor, because the power factors in the hierarchy are much more fraught with actual danger for black people than for whites.

The subject of manners has provided much grist for the South's mythology mill, most of it derived from general assumptions about putative codes of conduct governing social interaction between belles perpetually dressed in evening dresses and swirling ball gowns and the gentlemen who court and admire them and hope to get on their dance cards; from the idea of belles too fine for the exigencies of mere biology, of gentlemen too cultured to allow any slight to manners to go unchallenged, of swaggering formal gestures, of honor defended with blood if necessary. More generally, the myth seems to be fixated on those rules governing males' and females' expectations of each other. What the mythology sees as manners, however, is not manners at all but rather some excrescence of a more formal and rule-driven etiquette gleaned from *Gone with the Wind* and other fictions in which southern men have no life other than dancing or fighting, and southern women have no life at all except at dress balls.

Southern manners are both more and less complicated than this myth allows. In the first place, southern manners are not an elaborately defined or codified etiquette. There are no formal "rules" of the sort that seem to govern, say, Edith Wharton's fastidious and moribund New

York world, no ritual traditional gestures to admire and applaud from one generation to the next, as though southern life were a sort of long-run Kabuki performance; where these kinds of etiquettes exist in the South, they have more to do with class than with region, with social pretension than with the general behavior we think of as southern manners.

Southern manners are in fact the very antithesis of rules and of elaborate, self-conscious gestures. Southern manners can't even survive where too many rules exist because rules would choke off the spirit of the enterprise, and the spirit is manners' governing principle, their *raison d'être*. Paradoxically manners can thrive where *no* rules exist, because in the presence of social chaos they offer the mannersable an anchor in stability, a firm grip on character and behavior, and a self-justifying and too often self-serving vantage from which we can view the foibles of the unmannersable. Al Capp might have called southern manners a sort of "upright gland" that helps us keep honorable though all else fail about us. Thus our manners are intimately related to our morality, except that our manners are not so prescriptive.

Though southern manners are by no means passive, at their best they are almost exclusively responsive: they are infinitely flexible and highly sensitive to situation. They are based in two very general considerations —not principles: *considerations*: age before youth, women before men. The former is *by far* the more important. But even these general considerations operate on a finely calibrated sliding scale which permits class, gender, race, and wealth to intersect in ways that allow immediate and subtle and very nearly intuitive reconfigurations of the priorities.

Most southerners that I know of do not concern themselves over-much with the priorities of place or precedence that the two general considerations articulate. In practice the "priorities" are mostly general guidelines for helping us know in advance of need such practical things as who will go through a door first (since obviously not everybody can go through a door at the same time), who will be served first, who will get first consideration for vests or lifeboats when the liner goes down, who will get to sit down if there aren't enough chairs in the parlor: there needn't be any discussion of these things unless, for example, a younger man has a need for the one remaining chair—if he were holding a child, for example, or eating, or exhausted, or on crutches—or a child is in need of a lifejacket, in which cases almost any older woman would yield the chair or the lifejacket without even the remotest thought that manners had been breached.

Southern manners, then, operate as a general commitment to *niceness*; they anticipate and head off if possible any sort of rupture in the fabric of whatever interaction is taking place; there's more than a joke involved in some southerners' description of the Civil War as "the late unpleasantness"! It may be useful to think in the singular: not "southern manners" but *the southern manner*, the goal of which is first of all to avoid such ruptures and then, if avoid them we cannot, to ignore them: it is much worse form to laugh at or comment on or even to admit that you noticed the loud fart at the dinner table than it is to do the farting. One of southern manners' prime requirements, then, is to treat bad manners as if they were good manners or at least unavoidable accidents, like the fart: we reserve comment, if any, for later. White trash identify themselves as trash not at all because of their economic circumstances but because of the ways their behavior calls attention to itself and therefore to themselves. Of any sort of trashy behavior, my grandmother used to say: "It's just ignorance."

The need to avoid dealing straightforwardly with bad manners or aggressive behavior—that is, to avoid conflict—is both the defining strength and the debilitating weakness of the southern manner, and in practice they are often hard to distinguish, for the thoughtful and the observant, especially for the self-analytical southerner, and even more especially when manners get practiced in situations of hierarchy, wherein the thoughtful and analytical may always wonder whether their own display of manners is indeed manners, a knuckling under to the structure, or simply a necessary operating procedure.

That is, when manners operate in a public as opposed to a familial venue, they often do so under the terms of an implicit contract of noblesse oblige, according to which two or more parties of unequal position agree to act as though there are no differences between them; more specifically, they agree to act as though the differences do not matter, when in fact they matter very much. The contract, which obligates the higher person to be courteous, also obligates the lower person to courtesy; it is that responsive upward motion, the acquiescence of the lower person to the hierarchy, that ensures the smoothness of the encounter, that may or may not get the lower person what he or she wants out of the encounter. For both, then, manners are not just social largesse and goodwill dispensed in trickle-down or -up altruism, they are a specific, even if not conscious, investment in the social order: the manners of those higher obligate those lower to return the favor by "respecting" their "superiors." Especially in the public venue, then, southern manners reify social hierarchies, and they do so when those lower in the hierarchy accept the terms of the hierarchy and return the noblesse oblige with courtesies of their own. In racial and gender relationships particularly, they function most effectively when those lower in the hierarchy actually believe in the order that the hierarchy creates, believe that they are located in the hierarchy exactly where they ought to be, and are willing to defend with their lives the very social structure that keeps them in the lower position.

Obviously, manners can be instruments of aggression, even passive aggression. We all know the ones who make the elaborately self-conscious gestures of manners that are more designed to call attention to themselves than actually to facilitate encounters. When they do so, they become mannerisms rather than manners, a parody of the southern manner. Of course mannerisms, manner, and manners are not mutually exclusive;

they exist simultaneously in the same person, sometimes in the same gesture. Mannerisms are the aggressive form that southern manners take. By calling attention to themselves, they make explicit the obligations of those receiving the mannersable behavior: because I am mannersable toward you, you are obligated to be mannersable toward me, even though I am foreclosing on your mortgage or firing you; you have this obligation, quite simply, because I have economic power and you may need to borrow money from me again some day. When mannerisms operate, the dynamic in any encounter is that of raw power, which highlights and reinforces unequal relationships rather than ignoring them. Since the contract of noblesse oblige functions most powerfully when the contract is implicit rather than explicit, the elaborate self-conscious mannerism will be either aggression (if you are higher) or abasement (if you are lower); under these circumstances, the mannerism becomes a threat, an actual challenge, to the niceness that ordinarily governs any encounter: manners with an edge. Pleasantness has a hard time functioning in any encounter where power and weakness deal with each other as power and weakness; in such cases, even pleasantness, niceness, becomes a mannerism and a crude form of aggression.

Because Picayune's class distinctions were not very rigid, the protocols of noblesse oblige did not operate with much virulence. You could easily distinguish financial top from financial bottom, but the gradations in between were in some ways so fine as to be unidentifiable. The wealthy banker or merchant in suit and tie is happy to open the door for, or to share a cup of coffee or an afternoon's conversation with, the less wealthy one, with the merchant in khakis or chinos or the farmer in overalls, to whom he wants to lend money, sell something, or even just work with on a civic or church project. They may share a pew in church or have children in the band or on the football team. Unless they are old friends, they are likely to refer to each other formally as Mr. Jones and Mr. Smith, though if their social and financial differences are really marked, and especially if they have already done a good deal of business together, the older and wealthier may well refer to Smith by his first name, Ed, and Ed can presume to refer to Jones as Mr. Bill. If Ed works for Mr. Bill, he is likely to be pleased and flattered that Mr. Bill knows his first name and is willing to use it, and Mr. Bill uses it precisely to shower friendship and esteem upon his employee. But neither Ed nor Mr. Bill is under any delusion about their positions in the hierarchy and Ed is unlikely to violate the protocols by calling him anything but Mr. Bill, even when referring to him in the company of others. In fact, Ed knows that referring to his boss as Bill in the presence of others is likely to make him seem pretentious, uppity, and he knows that to refer to him to others as Mr. Bill will suggest a stronger and more believable relationship—that Mr. Bill trusts and believes him a good person, without actually offering friendship or social equality—than to call him Bill.

Only a few black customers referred to my father as Mr. Polk. Most called him Mr. Firestone, or Mr. Earl if they were old customers. Nearly all the white customers, at least those roughly my father's age, called him Earl, and he mostly returned the favor; if they were very old, he would call them Mr. Smith, unless he had known them for a long time, and then he would call them Mr. John. There were some white customers, not just trash, who called him Earl, to whom he would not return the first-name favor, because he wanted to keep a more formal distance. All the white customers called me Noel; all the black ones referred to me, when they had to, as Mista Noel, Young Mista Fi'stone, or simply: You Mista Fi'stone's boy? I tended to call older and/or wealthier adults, and those I knew in professional capacities—my teachers, say—by Mr. or Mrs. or Miss, though if I knew them well, I could presume to call some Mr. Floren or Mr. Willy. I called all black people by their first names and I would occasionally slip in a Ma'am or Sir, most often out of the habit of so addressing older people, without being conscious of violating a taboo, and certainly not, until I was much older, doing so deliberately.

The Picayune Rotary Club, of which my father was a proud member, made an elaborate ritual, at its weekly lunch meeting, of eliminating, even ridiculing, class and age differences among its members by assessing fines of one dollar upon any member for each time he called another member by anything other than his first name; they had a hilarious, even giddy, time under the heading of New Business accusing fellow members of instances of such misconduct. My father refused to call Claiborne McDonald Sr., the club's oldest member and a former mayor of Picayune, anything but Mr. McDonald. "I respect him too much," he said. "I'll just pay the dollar if I have to say anything to him." He would have fiercely objected to any implication that McDonald was higher than he on any scale but his age, and I'm not sure how McDonald's time as mayor factored into my father's attitude; but age would have been enough even if there were no other factors, and since McDonald was in no social or financial position to affect my father's life very much, there was a kind of purity about his show of respect (McDonald owned the local funeral home, so I guess there was a chance, a final one, for him to directly affect my father's life—in the leaving it). For the most part, their interaction was limited to the weekly Rotary meetings; whether a closer relationship would have allowed my father to call him Claiborne or even Mr. Claiborne, I'm not sure; both would have claimed, or implied, an intimacy he did not have.

As I say, of the two general considerations—age before youth, women before men—the former is by far the more important. In point of fact, except in the southern myth, manners have very little to do with gender relationships, except incidentally. More important than either, and of which these considerations are functions, are the much larger issues of niceness and smooth surfaces. I take here two highly mythologized southern examples, the practice of opening doors for ladies, and of saying Ma'am and Sir, which are often cited as being peculiarly southern forms of "manners."

I confess: I plead guilty to both. I pepper all my oral interaction with Sir and Ma'am: they are almost speech tics. But the question is not whether I use them when addressing my elders and/or superiors: I do. I use them almost indiscriminately with everybody—my elders, my colleagues, my students, my children, even very young children—not to express a relative position in the noblesse-oblige hierarchy nor even necessarily to express respect for a particular person, and in fact I can utter them in such a way as to express genuine contempt. What they express is a general respect for the idea of discourse, of human interaction, and for the possibility that I might enjoy and/or profit from a conversation with the person I am addressing; it posits a specific receptivity to such conversation. My use of Sir and Ma'am is ingrained behavior, very nearly instinctive. It's mostly—*mostly*—a matter of aesthetics: it really grates, rasps, on my refined sensibilities to ask a question and be greeted with *What?* or, more crudely, *Huh?*, and I assume, extrapolating from my own refinements, that they grate on other people's nerves too, and so work against communication, against niceness. These blunt monosyllables do not, to my ear, invite conversation or friendship; they say How dare you interrupt me? Ma'am and Sir, although monosyllabic, simply sound better, *nicer* to me, and work to prime the pump of conversation, smooth the hard surfaces of communication. I grant, of course, a very tender ear, but I *always* notice it when other people, especially children and students, don't use them, and I have to make a minor adjustment of my sonar to remind myself that mine is actually a stodgily oldfashioned if not completely quaint sensibility in these matters and that the offending party hasn't necessarily intended any disrespect or offense.

Likewise, I am an unreconstructed door-opener, and again the question is not whether I will open a door for a lady. Of course I will: I by God will open doors for anybody, for everybody, regardless of age, gender, race, creed, or color: show me a door and I will get to it first, and you better not get in my way. Like using Sir and Ma'am, I open doors almost instinctively, so automatically that as I have gotten older I have actually had to teach myself how to recognize, and yield to, those situations in which it is more appropriate for somebody to open the door for me, to one who expects to open the door for me because I am older, a professor, or a guest. I sometimes get caught with my mindless politesse showing between classes, and find myself functioning as a doorman for long lines of students in ingress or egress; I stand there until it dawns on me that I might have more important things to do, like get to class, for example. I also notice who says Thank you and who doesn't.

iii.

More melancholy reflection suggests that the best way to understand the southern manner is to think of it as a symptom of a neurosis rooted in a protestant theology that insists upon self-effacement, upon a denial of your own needs in favor of those of others, whether they are others' actual needs or your presumptions of them. The essential *act* of southern manners, the southern manner, then, is self-abnegation, invisibility. Though the gesture-symptom may be opening a door or giving up a seat on the bus or in the living room or in the lifeboat or rising when a lady stands, that gesture springs from a more basic, ingrained need to sacrifice our own desires or needs in favor of another's. The operating premise, the unarticulated assumption out of which all the gestures flow, is that you must not call attention to yourself in any way, either by farting at the dinner table or by noticing that somebody else has.

At its best, this assumption grants southerners a kind of Negative Capability, a vantage from which we can observe without being observed—a powerful position, which we can attain only if we overcome the pathology of its origins and understand it as a position instead of a condition. Many nonsoutherners mistake the southern manner as weakness or lack of intelligence. But a southerner can watch you and take careful aim, smiling and tolerating your bad manners, opening doors for you and saying Yes, Ma'am and Yes, Sir to your patronizing assumptions while you expose yourself as a shootable target. You assume because I'm nice that I'm also slow-witted and don't know how to use the gun. But I do. I'm not Forrest Gump, though that's the way you often treat me: I'm Columbo, and I have the advantage of you if you think of me as simpleminded and clumsy (not that we southerners have ever, as a group, benefitted much from the advantage). To be sure, some of us *are* slow-witted and can't, or at least are reluctant to, shoot or take advantage. This may only mean that you don't have anything we want or that we are continuing to be nice in spite of your appalling behavior; but it may also mean that the capability of negation has become the actuality, in which case the southern manner is indeed a neurotic condition imbedded not in breeding or character but rather in the vacuum where character ought to be, a black hole in an ego driven by a need for love and acceptance and approval which "proper" self-effacing behavior might purchase. We are thus easily, terrifyingly, vulnerable to anybody who offers to fill that vacuum, with love or tyranny or both. This condition is the dark underbelly of southern manners, perhaps of the southern manner itself.

One Baptist Son

AN ANATOMY: NOTES OF A SURVIVOR

Jesus was the answer,
but Elvis was the King.
—DIAMOND RIO

Jesus is the answer.
What was that question?
—COMMON GRAFFITI

J ESUS IS LORD OVER PICAYUNE: Thus saith signs that mark both entrances to Picayune from the interstate. It was mostly true when I lived there thirty-five years ago, and I suppose it's still mostly true—even though Picayune in the eighties acquired a reputation as one of the main drug distribution points in south Mississippi, so that one friend has suggested that Jesus is more nearly Drug Lord over the area. I don't know whether that's true or not, but I wouldn't be surprised: the town is well located along the interstate, large enough to attract a good deal of traffic from the hinterlands but sufficiently small that it can't support a very large or sophisticated police force. If it is true, Picayune would merely be continuing the long regional tradition of commerce in contraband: Pearl River County and environs were rumored to be major suppliers of moonshine whiskey to Chicago and other large cities during Prohibition, one of several such counties throughout the South that gave rise to facts and myths about the association between Baptists and moonshiners.

It would no doubt be more "southern" if I could write in scathing and bitter repudiation of my legacy from the Southern Baptist church I grew up in, if I could entertain with funny or tragic stories of small-town Elmer Gantrys, recall a cast of religious cripples with funny double names out of Flannery O'Connor, a locustlike plague of hellfire evangelists, or any of the various other strains of religious virus—ranging from glaring hypocrisies to the sorts of whimsical ironical recognitions contained in the epigraphs to this piece—that southern literature and mythology are so full of. There's plenty to repudiate, to be sure, but what's at issue in Southern Baptist life is something much more inimical than hypocrisy or grotesqueness. The cartoonlike grotesques and hypocrites and theogogues of the popular imagination bear about as much resemblance to the reality of Southern Baptist church life as the old Bible portraits of Satan with tail, horns, and trident bear to the nature of evil. Southern Baptist doctrine is much more problematical, even, than the simpler doctrinal questions about the existence of God or of an afterlife or the virgin birth or Christ's divinity—questions I happily leave to others. Critics who shoot at Baptist hypocrisy can easily hit a large but meaningless target, and miss the point entirely.

I'm rather concerned here with the ways in which Baptist doctrines and practice appropriate divinity, shape it to Baptists' own social and psychological ends, and the place of the individual within that shaping. Baptist theology is a complex system, both fragile and fortresslike, enervating and empowering, that insists upon an ideal of belief and behavior so impossibly high—perfection—that life within it is necessarily a constant series of evasions and deceits; hypocrisy may even be the only healthy reaction to the preposterousness of such a high standard.

Baptist theology is based in an epistemology that functions almost like a parallel universe. Baptists perforce have one foot—a toe or a hand, maybe—in this world's biology and history but everything else exists in another world altogether, one that allows little or no recognition of this world except as a drag on the other: that one toe or hand over here will cause disaster in the other and so our biblical instructions are, simply, to chop it off: "And if thy right eye offend thee, pluck it out . . . . if thy right hand offend thee, cut it off, and cast *it* from thee: for it is profitable for thee that one of thy members should perish, and not *that* thy whole body should be cast into hell" Matthew 5:29–30).

The system is so powerful as to function almost independently of human agency; in some ways even the hypocrites and theogogues are simply functionaries in the system's machinations to keep itself firmly in place and, lacking hypocrites and theogogues, the system itself would produce them. Throughout this meditation, then, whenever I speak of "Baptists" or "Baptist theology," I do not mean to judge any individual within the Baptist or any other fundamentalist system. I rather mean to discuss the system itself, which, though necessarily administered by human hands, has very little to do with human beings; indeed, the hypocrites and theogogues are perhaps the most victimized of all.

Baptist theology is based in blindness: I do not mean merely that blindness to the social constructions of race and gender and class for which we have lately become so well known, or even the fearful, willful blindness to human nature that makes Baptists unable to think rationally about something as natural as sexual desire, much less something as reasonable as, say, sex education. Willful blindness could be corrected by changing the will; Baptists appropriate the will long before it has any chance to exercise anything resembling freedom. Baptist theology is based in a world view that simply reverses itself, like a photo negative: it is a blindness that believes itself vision, a bondage that believes itself freedom, a poverty that believes itself abundance, a death that believes itself life.

Though I speak as a survivor, or at least as one in recovery—remission perhaps—I do so recognizing the full complexity of all social organization and want to make it clear at the outset that whatever troubles I had then and have since had with the Baptist system, my experience of *the people* of First Baptist, Picayune, was entirely positive. My memories are of middleclass people with a genuine sweetness of temperament, selfless manners, and a sincere wish to practice what Jesus taught—I mean, of course, what they were taught Jesus taught. In fact, First Baptist of Picayune was full of warm and loving folks, friendly and outgoing, open and generous: Paul Jenkins, my Sunday school teacher who owned the Red & White Food Store; Paul Padgett, music director at the church, who ran a good choir and taught me how to sing tenor; Vonceil Page, Ernie Stewart, Julia Calvin, the singing sisters Jo Ann Newman and Audie Harmon, Miss Mae Mitchell, Miss Jesse Stuart, and lots of others, who may have wrestled privately with a variety of demons or neuroses but didn't do so publicly enough for me to notice.

I note two mostly generic aberrations that vaguely disturbed without really disrupting the smooth texture of this moral placidity: one Sunday school teacher, my doctor for about a year, who ran away with his nurse; and one of the church stalwarts, a sweet and gentle woman, omnipresent at all church functions, who was married to the owner of one of the popular bars just across the Pearl River from us, in Louisiana. I never met the husband, that I remember. But she didn't seem to treat the fact as a cross to bear, though God knows what she thought privately; nor, so far as I could tell, did anybody else think much beyond the sad spiritual dimensions of the problem of her being, in the biblical language, "unequally yoked" with an unbeliever; her "situation" certainly didn't affect her interaction with other church members. But these were the only anomalies I remember among the church folks. I didn't experience the First Baptist Church as a hotbed of hypocrisy, of frustrated old maids or bachelors either with private lives at gossipy odds with public personae. Surely there were stories I didn't hear; but it has to be significant that I didn't hear them.

It is true that we opposed integration in the fifties, but we handled even that in ways that were mannersable and nonconfrontational. The deacons, of whom my father was one, and who discussed the policy with me, believed firmly that black people didn't any more want to worship with white people than white people wanted to worship with them, that all they wanted, really, was to be able to go where they were excluded. During crisis years, official church policy was to have deacons stationed at each entrance of the church, to greet black visitors at the door and politely escort them to seats the church had designated for them. The assumption was that seeing no resistance to their presence they would go away: under the circumstances of that terrible time and from their point of view, given the alternatives, it was a sane and sensible policy that seems to have worked. The walls of First Baptist, Picayune, were never breached, never challenged. Don't tell me it wasn't enough; I know that.

The people of First Baptist were, finally, as decent an assembly of human beings as can be found anywhere. They treated me with respect and love and gave me all the community and the nurture they could muster. Quite a lot: not enough, as it turned out, but that was the system's doing, perhaps my own doing, and not theirs.

The First Baptist Church of Picayune was, in the fifties, a huge, rambling white wood building full of intricate and devious stairways and stairwells, nooks and crannies holding wonderfully hidden odd-shaped rooms where we had Sunday school and youth meetings, and a huge auditorium of oak pews facing the choir and the pastor; a balcony overhung on three sides. The church faced the boulevard, its front entrance a huge imposing building-wide set of painted-gray concrete steps that led up to the front doors through four columns to the auditorium on the second floor. Sometime in the fifties we built a new brick building to the west side, along with a chapel for prayer meetings and other such occasions, mostly financed from money donated by L. O. Crosby Jr. It was two-storey and connected to the main building by a walkway; there was an elevator in the new building! We had five or six hundred members, and were by far the largest church in town, both in building size and in membership. We were mostly middle class, though with a sprinkling of really poor folks, and the Crosbys.

The pastor was John R. Maddox, D.D.—a Doctor of Divinity, an honorary, not an earned doctorate, though we were pleased to call him, and he was doubtless pleased to be called, "Dr. Maddox." Most of the church folks called him "Brother Maddox." I'm not sure I ever heard anybody call him "John." His sermons were full of homily and instruction for daily living, though he could throw himself into an evangelistic fervor and did fairly regularly remind us all that the real business of church was to win souls for Christ. To that end he would occasionally preach the traditional fire-and-brimstone sermon for which Baptists are so well known. When he got fervent and evangelistic, of course, he was preaching almost entirely to the converted; he invoked our totem, the suffering Jesus, and affirmed us in our communal life, in our differences from all the lost souls who were not of us. When on those occasions someone did accept Christ and join our flock, we were even more powerfully affirmed in our oneness: others want what we have, even if they don't always know it. Mostly he just instructed us, from the scripture, in how to live.

Once or twice a year Brother Maddox brought in a fire and brimstone evangelist for a revival. One was particularly effective, a dynamo from Florida who came to Picayune for a week and preached powerfully on heaven and hell—mostly, of course, on the latter. I never heard such perfervid eloquence about the terrors of hellfire than he preached, including one masterpiece of a sermon in which he described a visit to an emergency room to minister to a young man about to die from severe burn wounds: hell was never more vivid. He preached sermons that

made even the most unredeemable of reprobates among us go forward
to dedicate or "rededicate" their lives to Jesus. I still have the church
bulletin announcing that he would come to town, his picture adorning
the front. He is young, crewcut, a visionary, his eyes locked firmly on
the future: only now do I note that those visionary eyes seem slightly
crossed. Less than a year after he was in Picayune, we heard that he had
quit the ministry and run off with his secretary.

Lots of evangelists came to First Baptist. I'm sure pastors invited
their friends, that they all worked in various circuits among friends that
they made in college and at the seminary; these were mostly pastors at
other churches, and we allowed our pastor and music director to accept
invitations to a certain number of revivals per year in other churches. We
paid them with "love offerings," money especially collected during the
week for that purpose. Sometimes evangelism could be quite lucrative.
During the summer between my freshman and sophomore years at
Mississippi College I led the music at a revival in a small country church
just outside Brookhaven, Mississippi. I was paid $200 for my labors for
the week, a sum I thought more or less miraculous until I learned that
the evangelist had made over $2,000 for the same week.

The most interesting revivals at First Baptist, Picayune, however,
were conducted not by pastors but by professional evangelists. Some, like
Angel Martinez, were well known for their fiery pulpit style; the best were
those with a gimmick. One showed slides as he preached. (I was lucky:
I got to sit in the balcony and change the slides when he gave me the
signal—a part of things, I was!) He spent the week advertising that *one
night*—he wouldn't say which—he was going to show us *A PICTURE
OF JESUS CHRIST, AN ACTUAL PHOTOGRAPH OF THE SAVIOR!*
We were skeptical, but who could resist? He might have been hawking
indulgences or fragments from St. Peter's ulnae, but we would have
hung around to see. On the final night he showed us a slide of the
stains on the Shroud of Turin, which indeed do look like a portrait

of somebody. Another evangelist played a trombone solo during the offering. Yet another billed himself as the flying evangelist; he flew from town to town in his own little Piper Cub and promised a free flight to anybody who got saved.

The best preacher I ever heard, though, was R. G. Lee, retired pastor of Bellevue Baptist Church in Memphis and renowned for a sermon called "Payday Someday," a ripping hour-long fabulous spellbinding disquisition on the domestic and civic squabbles of Ahab and Jezebel. He was to preach it on Saturday night of the revival, and throughout the week he advertised it from the pulpit: he had preached it several hundred times, he said (he had an exact figure; I can't remember it), and he offered to sell us a color film of it.

He and the sermon were so well known among Southern Baptists that the church was packed on Saturday night: Baptists from all over, professors and students from the New Orleans Baptist Seminary, came for the event, and it was a show, well worth the trip. It was a hot summer Saturday night long before we had airconditioning, and the number of bodies in the church made the air almost fetid, even with all the ceiling fans running. As Lee spoke Ahab and Jezebel materialized before us: no woman was ever wickeder than she, no king ever more perfidious than he; no two sinners ever reached a more fitting or inevitable end: *Payday Someday.* Lee told their story with consummate pulpit artistry. Building to his well-rehearsed climax, he narrated how Jehu's soldiers threw Jezebel out of her tower window. He leaned his tall body far over the pulpit and traced her fall through the air with his finger from the balcony to the front of the pulpit, then pointed to where she lay, broken and bleeding, at the feet of those in the first row. He paused for a perfectly-timed dramatic moment and then pronounced her doom; his eyes flared and his big jowls shook and his guttural-gravelly voice was splendidly a-rage with the thrilling appropriateness of her end: *"And the dogs—came—and—licked—up—her—bloooood!"*

We were transfixed by that image and by his voice, which hung almost visible in the hot air around us. He paused long enough for his voice to appropriate that air, to make it his, so that he controlled our very breathing. Then he asked us all to stand for the invitation, to sing "Just as I Am," while those with decisions to make came forward to take the pastor's hand. He had preached for over an hour and so with the preliminaries we had already been there an extraordinarily long time, even for Baptists, even for revivals. It was a long invitation. We had standing jokes about the ninety-nine verses of "Just as I Am"; there were only six, but it was common during revivals for congregations to sing them over and over as long as people were coming down the aisle to repentance or as long as the preacher felt there might be "someone out there who feels God working at his heart, someone out there who needs to make a decision tonight; right now, come on, while we sing another stanza."

This night's invitation was as extraordinarily long as the sermon and the occasion, and we stood in the heat, singing and being fervent for at least a half hour after the sermon was over, Lee stopping the singing every so often to inject another call for folks to be saved. During one such pause in the singing, he adjured us all to think that this might be the last chance—the *last chance*—we'd ever have to accept Jesus, that we might not even be able to walk out of this church tonight. As he compelled us with those words, Mike Hodgson, a Presbyterian friend standing by me in a back corner of the auditorium, fainted from the heat: he fell with a crash that sent shudders through the entire church. Lee, I say with some admiration, had the grace not to say "See! See! What did I tell you?" but everybody in that building thought of mortality, of eternity. Mike was humiliated but unharmed, and shrugged it off with a Presbyterian sort of fatalism. Since the church was full of preachers, professors, and other believers (if there had been mere sinners in Picayune wanting to get in they wouldn't have found a seat), I doubt that the incident had a serious impact on the number of souls saved.

Because I was a "preacher boy" and sort of underfoot around the church, I claimed an amateur's right to meet this famous pro, even assumed he'd be happy to meet and encourage an aspiring pulpiteer. Early in the week I stayed around after one of the morning services to get Brother Maddox to introduce me. He did. Lee did a take, adjusted his glasses to look down at me, and turned away without a flicker of interest in a teenager. It was my first experience with religious pride, but by no means my last.

I am still something of a student of good preaching. I know the language, the style, the content of most of the topics as they are announced, and I can still watch television preachers with some—well, not so much pleasure as, say, lingering professional interest in the quality of the performance, which allows me to indulge some nostalgia for something, I'm not sure what, that remains constant even through my repudiation. I miss the three or four minutes a week I spent with Jimmy Swaggart of a channel-flicking Saturday night before his fall from grace and I am still fascinated with radio preachers. I have great affection for the hymns and the gospel songs, especially gospel quartets of the Stamps-Baxter style. I can still sing the melody and the three lines of harmony for most of the hymns in the *Broadman Hymnal* and I still remember most of the words.

It is more pleasant than I can say to end an evening with other survivors standing around a piano, bourbon in hand, singing old hymns, especially if the pianist is a survivor too who remembers all the old revival runs and glissandos, the thunderous double- and triple-chord scales and descants, not to mention the fervor and the urgency of those times, of that life; such evenings are especially pleasant if there is a Catholic or an infidel or a foreigner or, on good occasions, a Yankee present who has no idea what fraternity, other than Baptist, we are part of. Perhaps the pleasure, in watching and singing, comes from a survivor's irony. Perhaps it's from touching base with the securities of the old foundations, even if the memories are more secure than the foundations ever were. Perhaps we're mesmerized, like those once bitten staring at the cobra in the zoo's glass cage, safely out of striking distance but poised to strike yet again should the glass go down or prove to be an illusion.

ii.

Baptists have well earned all and more of our reputation for closed-mindedness, especially of late, since nouveaux-riches Pentecostal and Assembly of God preachers and churches have elbowed their way, via televangelism, into the economic mainstream of middle- and lower-middleclass protestantism where Baptists once reigned supreme: whence Baptists have begun to try to out-fundamental them. With this formidable competition, Baptist leaders have turned their traditionally passive limitation of vision—an actual refusal, during the civil rights years especially, to take an active political stand—into a more aggressive agenda of intolerance and intervention in public life and private lives. I watched with some horror and bemusement—that cobra—when a friend (as much a friend, at any rate, as you can be with somebody who had been as touched by the Holy Ghost as he thought he was) from my years at Mississippi College became president of the Southern Baptist Convention and led the charge, right into the Bush White House, against homosexuals, abortions, and other assorted crimes against nature and nature's God. He came out foursquare for prayer in the public schools and a return to family values, and encouraged the suspicion of professors at Southern Baptist colleges and universities and seminaries who didn't toe a fundamentalist, literalist, theological line. As I watched, I was reminded of my friend Gary Stringer's pursuit of the word "fundamentalist" to its etymological den: it is derived from the word "fundament," which means "buttocks" or "anus." Clearly, Stringer opines, fundamentalist = asshole.

We were fundamentalists at First Baptist, Picayune, in the fifties, but it was not "fundamentalism" with the finely-honed edges of lunacy (Jim Bakker) or meanspiritedness (Pat Robertson and Jerry Falwell) or simple madness (Oral Roberts) that it now has, though I dare say that some of the evangelists who came through wouldn't have blanched at making a buck or two while saving souls had there been a cable satellite hookup: theirs was a limitation of technology rather than of ambition or imagination. To be sure, there were some assholes in the church, but more often than not that was incidental to religion, however accommodating religion was to it: it was something they brought with them when they came, took with them when they left.

We at First Baptist took pride in being fundamental in our under-standing and interpretation of the scriptures, though we didn't proclaim that pride too loudly because "fundamentalist" was a sort of generic term we used to refer, not flatteringly, to lower-class white churches that we often called "Holy Rollers" because of their highly emotional worship that we didn't want to be associated with: that was how rural and undereducated folks worshiped. We were "high church" at First Baptist, though we didn't use that term either because it smacked too much of Catholicism and Episcopalianism. We considered ourselves serious, rational, respectable, thoughtful students of the Word; we disdained equally the crass emotionalism of lower-class churches whose adherents spoke in tongues or healed by faith and the cold formality of the highly ritualized services of Catholicism and Episcopalianism. We would no more have handled snakes or spoken in tongues or danced in the aisles or tried to heal the sick than we would have worshiped Mary or genuflected to a cross. I recall only rarely anything as enthusiastic as applause. We steered a hightoned middle ground, expressing our emotion through hymnsinging, our formal worship through a church service as ritualistic in its procedures and rhetoric as any Catholic service could have been, though of course we denied that it was ritualistic because we didn't kneel during the service or recite paternosters or Hail Marys or make the sign of the cross: outrageous and mysterious acts, not biblically authorized, and so of the devil.

Southern Baptists deny that we are Protestant. We teach that as a body we were never part of the Roman Catholic Church; we proudly trace our spiritual and theological heritage in a straight undeviating line directly back to Christ; we maintain that we alone have been completely true to Christ's teachings; we did not dilute the power or meaning of Christ's message by veering off through St. Peter into Mariolatry or other forms of idolatry or intercession. Thus we proclaim that *we* are the one true scriptural Church, no matter what Catholics say.

The distinction of being the one *true* church is a crucial one for Baptists, because being right is central to the enterprise of being saved. To the outsider, such doctrinal quibbling may seem pointless, but to the insider nothing less than eternal life hangs in the balance; being right (not doing, I say: being) is precisely the point, the only point, the one point that does matter. Being right is the most important unofficial sacrament of fundamentalism; its two official sacraments are mostly adjuncts to it, and even they usually function more to define our differences from others than to celebrate or commemorate their essential meaning.

Baptists have only two sacraments, baptism and the Lord's Supper: we observed them at least once a quarter. We never called the Lord's Supper Communion (that too was a high churchism, to be eschewed by the unpretentious), except in the doctrinal phrase "Closed Communion," which meant that the Lord's Supper, like baptism, should only be partaken of by those who had been saved; Methodists, I believe, had Open Communion. As understood by and practiced in Baptist churches, however, these two sacraments are riven by flat contradictions that demonstrate the fundamental flaw in Baptist theology.

We insist on the one hand that we follow the Bible literally in baptizing by complete immersion, which is how Jesus was baptized—by John the *Baptist*—and so can claim that we are scripturally superior to other churches' symbolic practice of sprinkling. On the other hand, we insist just as vigorously—righteously—that the Lord's Supper is symbolic, since to be as literal in communion as we are in baptism would mean that we'd have to serve wine in church (not to mention, of course, agree that wine and other alcoholic beverages are scripturally acceptable). We ridiculed the Catholic doctrine of transubstantiation, though in doing so we tacitly admitted that on this point of doctrine Catholics are even more literal than we.

Most Baptist and fundamentalist arguments about literalism are, like these, really arguments about which scriptures people need help "understanding" and which are clear from the words on the biblical page. Understanding is not interpretation, of course; interpretation is not a spiritual exercise but an intellectual one and therefore idiosyncratic and liable to error. Baptists are good at this: we can argue with the same sweet smiles on our collective face that such Old Testament injunctions as those against working on the Sabbath and against women's cutting their hair need to be understood in their cultural contexts but that New Testament instructions to women to keep their proper inferior places and St. Paul's various animadversions against women and homosexuals do not.

Doctrinal intensity can easily descend to the minuscule, the petty. The First Baptist Church of a much larger city in Mississippi once nearly split over an issue raised when a committee was interviewing a candidate not even for the pastorate but for the lowly post of summer youth minister. One committee member asked the befuddled young man whether he were an a-millenialist, a pre-millenialist, or a post-millenialist. Obviously it was a question with a correct answer, though the poor candidate had no idea what any of the terms meant—nor would I have at his age, and I in fact had to look up the terms when I was told this story. Whatever answer he gave precipitated the proponents of the other two sides into some agitation over this important issue, and this large church nearly dissolved over what position it should expect a youth minister to hold: can't be too careful whom we put in charge of our children: might lead them to error. Some in this church often set a place at the dinner table for Jesus. I didn't know any at First Baptist of Picayune who did that sort of thing, and I recall no doctrinal disputes of that magnitude—of any magnitude, as a matter of fact. Most people at Picayune would have thought such disputations ridiculous.

As I say, such doctrinal pettifogging, such a felt need to separate ourselves from others with whom we might otherwise have a lot in common, must seem like so much windless smoke to people who haven't grown up in such a tradition. They are right: no wind blows clarity into the vision nor even shuffles the various degrees of smoky density around so that we might occasionally see at least some differing arrangements of darkness, light, and haze. Baptist theology is largely smoke gone solid; it is constructed of evasions of and diversions from logic and common sense. To be sure, religion is in its essence illogical, irrational; it has to be since it exists to explain and to provide grounds for human beings to negotiate with all the mysteries that govern our lives. The greatest of Christian theologians recognize this, and there is nothing wrong with a religion that is mysterious and illogical—that's what's best about the good ones.

But Baptist theology in practice does not recognize mystery, the unexplainable: it insists rather that it has hold of absolute certainty, Truth. It teaches that the Bible (if we know how to read it) can reveal to us everything we need to know; the more completely fundamentalist you are, the more completely you are likely to believe that it reveals *everything*, from the date of Armageddon to where the next president is to come from to the name and address of the Antichrist. Everything in fundamentalist theology works to deny mystery, to assure everybody that the unexplainable is in fact easily explained and that those things we don't understand now will eventually be revealed to us. At its worst, fundamentalist certainties trivialize religion's whole enterprise, from Jim Bakker's glib message, Send me money and you will be happy, to bumper stickers proclaiming that Things Go Better With Jesus. There is no best.

Nevertheless, Baptists make a good deal of faith's irrationality when it serves the purpose. When you point out even such elementary and nonthreatening contradictions of logic as that contained in the symbolic-literal practice of the Lord's Supper and baptism, Baptists will tell you that you are overintellectualizing, that some things have to be taken on faith: the fear of the Lord is the beginning of wisdom. Intellectuals should get in line with rich folks trying to get through the eye of that needle. Baptists are thus rabidly anti-intellectual, though we argue just the opposite, claiming loudly that real scientific inquiry will fully—eventually—confirm everything in the Bible, even if we have to wait to get to heaven for the confirmation. We dismiss intellectuals who challenge us by charging that they don't have the *true* wisdom, but we eagerly trot out the scientist who finds God in a test tube or under a microscope or in the stars or in the miracle of birth. Thus we don't have to deal with history or evidence or even our own experience, which are fluid, shifting, even volatile, subject to the motion of winds, and can't be True, because of course Truth is singular and unchanging: eternal. We block out rational thought because we begin not at ground zero of experience and meditation, but at ground so long past zero as to be smoked over into darkness with layers and layers of tradition and usage and denial and outright hogwash.

As an ideological structure, Baptist theology is complete down to every jot and tittle, to the disposition of the last sparrow; it is systematic, capable of explaining every question, forestalling every doubt, if you want it to. It is logical or at least, given its major premises and its sustaining evasion that what we don't understand now we must take on faith, able to dismiss illogicalities: it is sweeping, complete, unassailable, and fragile as an eggshell. For all its Gothic intricacies, its vaulting naves and apses and flying buttresses, its main strength is our fear of examining it: A Mighty Fortress Is Our God, but mightier still is our ignorance. What we propose as the container of our faith is the best evidence of our lack of it. Baptists, who claim access to ultimate power, are a fearful fearful people.

Baptist theology is essentially ideological: salvation doesn't depend on what you do, but rather on what you believe. Preachers harp on the scripture—"Believe on the Lord Jesus Christ and thou shalt be saved"— and prove conclusively and irrefutably through other scriptures that there is not one damned thing anybody can *do* to be saved, except believe. Just believe. The saved will behave "properly" but Baptist sermons were and still are rife with stories of thieves and murderers saved on deathbeds, at the last minute, by their faith at last in a loving Jesus, son of a loving God. But what, you are bound to ask, of those who get saved—accept Jesus— as children and then become blackguards and whoreson dogs in spite of it? Methodists, though usually more generous and tolerant in most things than Baptists, were less generous about this than Baptists were. Methodists could get saved but had to keep working at it: they could not gain salvation by good works but they could lose it by bad works. Baptists concocted a doctrine worthy of any Puritan divine, actually a sort of protective refinement of Calvinistic predetermination: once saved always saved, we claim. How could it be otherwise, with an omnipotent loving God? With his eye beyond time, God already knew that and precisely how you would backslide even when you took Jesus into your heart, and so how could he give you a gift that you already did not, could not, deserve, and which lack of desert he knew in advance you were fully going to justify? It's a comfort that saves us, finally, from our own unredeemable selves.

iii.

One of the central rituals of being "saved," of being "born again," in the Baptist church is the penitent's public "profession of faith" in Jesus. The public profession presumes that the penitent has already confessed his or her sins and has asked Jesus for forgiveness. For younger penitents, such confessions are usually made in a more private place, during consultation and counselling with the evangelist and/or Sunday school teacher and then with the pastor, perhaps during or just after a week-long revival when emotions (not to say pressures) are at fever pitch, and sometimes in the presence of one or both parents. There is no age limit, no theological "age of accountability"; the sincerity of the confession and the maturity of the penitent are left to the discretion of the counselling pastor. Children much younger than eleven or twelve are usually discouraged from making a profession of faith, but it is not unusual, in hard core fundamentalist churches, to see children much younger than this already "called" to the ministry and actively engaged in preaching. The penitent announces this confession to the church family by going down to the front of the church during a hymn of invitation at the end of a sermon, to face the congregation while the pastor or (in large churches) the associate pastor proclaims to all the nature of the penitent's "decision." The church then moves into the democratic formality of a business meeting when the pastor asks the congregation, "What is your will?" Some member, usually a deacon, responds "I move she be received," someone seconds, and the pastor calls for a vote: all in favor say "Amen." I never heard those opposed asked to vote, perhaps because there is no opposite to "Amen."

If the penitent is a young person, parents are asked to stand with him or her and face congregation of friends. After the benediction, the new church members stand at the front of the church while the congregation files by to shake their hands or hug them in welcome and affirmation. Once a quarter or so, more often if necessary, all those who have made such public professions during the previous period are baptized in a ceremony during one of the Sunday services. There are still small rural churches that baptize in nearby creeks and rivers and lakes, some by choice because that's where Jesus was baptized, some because they have no other place; but most churches have now built baptismal fonts into the area immediately behind the choir loft so that baptisms can proceed on schedule despite weather, say, and with no inconvenience—muddy shoes or a walk or drive to the riverside or a delay in getting home to dinner—to the members of the congregation. After being baptized, the new church member is entitled to partake of the Lord's Supper.

Though a good deal of Southern Baptist life is engaged with such public and communal displays of faith, a good deal more of it is inescapably a very private engagement with the fragmentations of doubt and isolation. For all the public display of communal certainty, the actual business of salvation remains very private, because of the Baptist doctrine of the priesthood of the believer. In dying for our atonement, this doctrine teaches, Christ became the mediator between each individual and God. Ministers may counsel us, may guide, cajole, plead, warn, frighten, harass us, and even pray for us; but they cannot intercede for us with God. That's our own scary business, and it is frightening indeed because for all the byzantine elaborateness of the theological "system," the scaffolding of certainty, we are finally left to our own devices. We have no scale by which to calibrate the proper amount of penance to be performed for absolution. That is, Baptists have no such penitential correlative to their sins as Catholics do, no quid pro quo measure by which any sin—impure thoughts, say—requires ten paternosters or Hail Marys to get it wiped off the ledger.

But such a scale would be useless to Baptists, because in practice Baptist doctrine does not differentiate one sin from another in terms of relative seriousness. There are *no* degrees of sin: all sins are equal in magnitude and equally odious in God's sight because they all testify to the lack of perfection that we were born with. To break one commandment is to break them all because, as pastors frequently explain, the Ten Commandments form a chain (apt metaphor) on which we hang, dependant, and, since no chain can possibly be any stronger than its weakest link, to break any one of the Commandments has the same effect as breaking them all.

The only scale we have to measure the seriousness of our sin is that provided by the stark contrast between the totality of our sinful nature and the perfection of Jesus' example; the only scale we have exacerbates rather than alleviates our miserable condition in sin. We therefore have no way to measure the efficacy of our faith and so no guideposts by which to measure the certainty of our salvation: no countable Hail Marys or rosaries, no priest to deliver extreme unction if necessary, to certify that all is forgiven, to speak out loud, where we can hear rather than just hope for, the clear comforting actual words: today shalt thou be in paradise. Baptists are therefore inescapably always alone with our venality, a terrible place to be: it's where everybody else is, of course, but it's particularly frightening to Baptists, because thanks to Jesus *we're not supposed to be there.*

Likewise, since for a man to look at a woman with lust in his heart is the same as committing adultery, it follows more generally that the very *desire* to do something sinful makes you just as guilty as if you had actually done it. In asking Jesus "to come into our hearts," then, Baptists ask him to help us avoid even thinking about committing a sin: in effect, we ask him to obliterate our own human nature. Baptists do not usually confess particular sins to pastor or parents (for the most part, parents and pastors don't want to know the particulars, even for a nine year old). We must rather confess a general—no: an absolute—condition of sinfulness, a predisposition to sin inherent in our nature and so constant in our daily lives that we have to be ever vigilant against anything that might lead us to indulge, or even desire to indulge, in some dalliance with this corrupt and corrupting world; living and being odious in God's sight are thus inextricable from each other. It's another pernicious symptom of the Baptist denial of the physical world, our fear of it, our need to repress it entirely. In this we are yet again unlike Roman Catholics, who build Mardi Gras into their system, a formal and even ritualistic recognition of desire, a spiritual steamletting.

It's always Lent in the Southern Baptist heart. In Baptist theory, if not in the practice of individual Baptists who actually go, Mardi Gras revelry is anathema, chaos, and to be despised because Baptists and other fundamentalists cling fiercely to certainty, the only raft in a fearsome sea of hormones and desires.

Fear implies doubt, doubt means lack of faith, and Baptists do not understand that faith, by definition, includes doubt, could not exist without it. Doubt rather makes our faith suspect if it does not cancel it out completely. We are in this way thwarted from the beginning, caught in a virtually escape-proof trap: the scriptures tell us about the fabulous power of faith, but also let us know, in precisely the same terms and at precisely the same moment, that we will, can, never have *enough* faith. Faith can move mountains, we are told jubilantly; even an amount as minuscule, as microscopic, as a mustard seed can *move mountains!!* So why can't I move mountains? Even though nobody in history or mythology or metaphor either has ever actually moved a mountain, the fact that I can't do it proves irrefutably that there must be something wrong with my faith, and so with me. The scriptures thus undermine faith in the very act of giving it; the gift of faith makes us impotent with the very tantalizing prospect of its power.

I'm not talking about the official rhetoric here: a pastor would tell us to remember that salvation is a gift, that all we have to do is accept it: to believe. The problem is with us, not with the system. But such assurances throw everything right back on us: the mustard seed of faith that we don't have gets transmogrified into a mountain of doubt that we do have and we can't move it either. Doubt may thus be for Baptists the unpardonable sin.

Baptists are bombarded daily with messages about our worthlessness. Salvation is a gift we don't now and can't ever deserve and can't work for. Even if we keep all the Ten Commandments, we still can't be certain of salvation. All we can be certain of is our own worthlessness, the main evidence for our need of salvation. The closest we can come to the certainty of salvation is the hope of it, which doubt transforms into intensity, faith's fervor, in the practice of its rhetoric and its rituals: the sinner not even in the hand of an angry God waiting to be dumped but, our foot already sliding, we are born plummeting deservedly toward hell and only our strength of will, habit, or language keeps us suspended, terrified, above the lake of fire that is our due.

The effort is exhausting because we know that what certainty we attain by the effort is an illusion, intensity's façade, a subterfuge, a holding pattern until certainty comes along. The degree of intensity exacerbates the degree of doubt that caused the intensity. Increasing amounts of intensity counter increasing amounts of uncertainty, until we are pulled apart by a growing abyss between the external effort of our fervor and our hope and the internal drag of doubt. Fanaticism is thus fueled by fear more than by faith.

People deal with this abyss with a sort of manic singlemindedness that in its most harmless manifestation makes people take signs on which they've printed the text of John 3:16 to football games to hold up for the television camera, as if that makes them witnesses for Christ; that at its nuttiest makes preachers scream at Bourbon Street revellers to repent; that at its most shameful and exploitative leads one charlatan to ask poor old people for their pensions so that they can help his TV network televise Jesus' Second Coming and another to claim that he has talked to a 900-foot-tall Jesus who says Send money; and that at its most pitiable leads those poor old people to send it.

iv.

My spiritual life during the fifties was not so much a struggle between the spirit and the flesh, though God knows adolescence was total war on both, as a struggle between what religion gave me and what it took away in the giving; between what it told me I needed and what it allowed me to have.

My parents took me to church every time the doors opened—Sunday morning, Sunday night, Wednesday night prayer meeting, and every day and night of any revival; others mostly came to Sunday morning services or to Sunday school and then went home before church, and were fairly ragged about even that. Even so, my parents were by no means sanctimonious or feverishly religious, and they, my father especially, held a class disdain for real fundamentalists, holy rollers and hardshells and even, to a lesser extent, for other Baptist churches that weren't *First Baptist*. My parents weren't particularly evangelistic, except in their willingness to give donations to support missionaries to China—the annual Lottie Moon Christmas offering—though I can't swear that they gave significant sums to that. They didn't drink, not out of strong religious conviction, but rather because there were alcoholics in my father's family and he didn't want to risk becoming one too. Every so often, perhaps after a revival or a particularly effective sermon, my father would reinstitute a family daily Bible-reading and devotional time ("The family that prays together stays together," John Maddox admonished us every Sunday); he would manage to hold us to it for a couple of days or so and then it would get sort of lost in the general ruck and rumble of our daily life. We did not talk a lot about religion in the house, or about Jesus, and even during the dead dark days after I became a ministerial aspirant, in the eighth or ninth grade (!), there was still some slight resistance to spiritual conversation, (as, it occurs to me now, to sexual conversation). They did not encourage me to become a minister, but they were very happy when I felt the "call" and were very supportive.

It was all very intense to me in Picayune, but I didn't experience the intensity as fanaticism and would have recoiled from the description. In my intensity, so far as I can tell, I was mostly alone among my peers, who seemed to have a much easier time with religion than I did, or at least got from somewhere a much more practical sense of its relation to reality. My friends worked their way through adolescence generally enjoying themselves in ways that frustrated me at the time, but which now, past all the clumsiness and the risk, seem to me much more sensible than my own lamentable (to me) sins of omission (all of them: I stand selfconvicted of every known sin of omission, and I probably made up some): Ah Sue! Ah Donna! Ah Marcia! Ah Carol! Ah Gaylene! Ah Sharon! what pleasures might we have shared, how different I might have been, had I not been washed so spotlessly in the blood, so filled with the spirit!

I've never been quite sure why my friends escaped and I didn't. I do not know what kinds of spiritual struggles they had, whether they had any. Most did not seem as compromised with reality as I was; Joe Ratcliff and Jack Wylie, both at the time also ministers-to-be, seemed as perfectly at ease with their faith as others did with their rebellion or their indifference. I did not find a larger community until I got to Mississippi College and ran into a hive of folks with problems similar to my own, though how many of us knew that what we had were "problems," I can't say. I thought at first that my fellow students confirmed me in my faith; I later learned that they mostly confirmed me in the problematics of intensity. They provided me a sufficiently large sample of people for me to believe, now, that my generalizations about the effects of the Baptist Church on the individual are more than just my whining about what it did to me. In the intervening years I have talked to dozens and dozens of students whose symptoms sound a lot like mine. And when I see on television today the faces, by turns orgiastic and utterly glazed over, of those who sit and listen to preachers spouting the same specious nonsense that I listened to as a teenager, I know how widespread the fundamentalist damage has been to our regional nervous system. But whether people in the South or anywhere else where fundamentalism has a hold deal with it by submitting, by rebelling, or by feigning indifference, make no mistake: the church defines the moral agenda against which they function.

The Southern Baptist Church was thus an intimate part of my life from the beginning. My grandfather and one of my uncles were preachers, my father a deacon. I myself accepted the "call" to preach very early in high school.

The idea of the "call" is, I gather, unique to fundamentalist churches. I don't know how people decide to become ministers in other denominations, but I know that Methodists, Presbyterians, and Episcopalian ministers move from church to church according to decisions made at organizational levels higher than the individual church. This always struck me as highly efficient but in lots of ways undesirable for the local church, especially if it liked its current minister and mourned when he was told to move on—as happened in Picayune when David Ulmer was rotated away from First Methodist. It was also often hard on minister's families, the constant moving, making new acquaintances; for their kids it was like being an army brat, I have been told.

Baptists do things differently; for all the elaborateness of the Southern Baptist Convention's structure, each church mostly maintains itself as an absolutely independent entity. People become church professionals by yielding to "God's will," and as professionals they move from one post to another not by the will of a bishop somewhere, but by God's will, a will expressed in a "call." In college we joked about it: long-distance rates from heaven, for example, and some of us noted the frequency with which God "called" pastors from smaller churches to larger churches with larger salaries and more prestigious pulpits. But there were enough examples of folks who accepted a downward call, to leave a large-church sinecure and head, with kids in tow, to the wilds of backwoods Africa or China: these were the ones who made it into the pantheon of our heroes, our occupational liturgy, the ones who confirmed us in the idea that God actually had a *plan* for all of our lives, a definite place for us. The ones who left high-profile pastorates to serve the meek and lowly in out-of-the-way places were all the proof we needed that God called people to the more politically powerful and advantageous churches too.

The "call" is God's direct, dramatic, intervention into our lives, a replication in local and personal history of Christ's intervention in human history. God leads. God directs. God controls. We submit. Through prayer we learn God's will for our lives. Through faith we act upon his will. He calls us to be a preacher, a missionary, a youth director, a musician—and to serve in secular occupations, too. Evidence of the call is our desire to serve in one of those capacities, often publicly expressed in uncontrollable tears of joy and submission.

Pastorless churches choose a "pulpit committee," who seek God's will and guidance through prayer and other contacts in the profession; committee members travel to other churches to hear nominees preach (unbeknownst to the nominee); if they like what they hear and feel led by God's spirit, they invite him to preach a "trial" sermon at their own church. If this preacher feels "led" by the spirit to explore this opportunity, he accepts the invitation to deliver the trial sermon. If the church feels led to offer him the pastorate, he and his family and perhaps friends and other advisers pray together to seek God's will. If God calls him, he accepts the new job. At some point in this process, I don't know when, the parties discuss salary and benefits packages, school systems, opportunities for wives, and other practical realities associated with any move. I suppose it varies from situation to situation how important such mundane matters are in the larger scheme of God's will.

High church—*First* Baptist—churches might allow the very young to profess a "call" to one of these religious professions at the end of a church service just as they would allow a child to profess faith in Jesus and be saved. They would also allow children, teenagers, to lead church services on special "youth nights" or lead the singing portions of the service and give a testimonial or even "preach" to the congregation on occasion, but would encourage such young folks toward a college and seminary education before allowing them actively to engage in the profession of religion—to be employed by a Southern Baptist church. Normally such a church would "license" a young person to preach— that is, officially approve his desire to serve in that capacity—before he left for college; at the end of his seminary training, the home church would then officially "ordain" him to the gospel ministry, an elaborate ceremony involving public discussions of doctrinal matters and a laying-on of hands by the deacons, a ritual wherein each of the church's deacons would stand before the praying candidate and literally lay hands on the candidate's head and shoulders, while offering his own silent prayer.

More extreme fundamentalist churches did not require college or seminary educations of their ministers and in more than one case, of which Marjoe is the most famous example, some denominations have actually offered nine-year-olds as performing evangelists to large revivals. The only requirement was that they be called of God, led by the spirit, and touched by some divine fire that gave them access to a Truth that education not only could not give them but might actually deny them.

In my case, I now know that the "call" gave me access to the community of First Baptist that I might not otherwise have had. My call elevated me to some special status in the eyes of the church folks. I felt, hoped, it would give me some special status at home that would force my father—not my heavenly one—to approve of me. I got affirmation, a sense of purpose, a place in the system.

From the time of my call until Christmas of my junior year in college, when I finally admitted that I didn't want to marry any woman that wanted to marry a preacher (this admission not coincidentally related to my current interest in a woman who didn't want to be married to one), I did my best to be a minister: I often preached at First Baptist's "mission" across the tracks, as it were, in a poor section of town, to as many as three to five people in the congregation. In high school I preached at two or three weekend youth revivals in local churches, others in college, and led the singing at several other revivals where others did the preaching. On numerous occasions during these years I served as a youth minister for weekend spiritual retreats, a job that involved entertaining the young folks, being a "dynamic young man," and, finally, "witnessing."

Perhaps people who knew me then would tell you different, because I only know how I looked to myself; but I do not believe that I was ever the fanatical monster of the popular imagination or a hypocritical hellmonger. Fanatics wore signs on Bourbon Street that proclaimed

I'M A FOOL FOR CHRIST
WHO'S FOOL ARE YOU?

I rather wanted to be a simple servant of the Lord—if, of course, I could do that in the course of getting my own self saved—wherever he wanted me to be, though I hoped and prayed he would not see fit to have me do these things in darkest Africa or among the Chinese: helping, counselling, consoling, marrying folks, seeing them into and out of this world, and giving them hope for the next. It seemed a simple thing to want.

I was fanatic, then, not as the zealot who constantly preaches or moralizes at or condemns everybody else, but in the sense that I took everything—*everything*—seriously and I was, like Jonathan Edwards, much more concerned with salvation than with living. Eternity always leaned in at me, beckoning and ominous, investing even the simplest deeds or thoughts with dire consequences. During one particularly fierce period of several years—most of my adolescence, actually—I dreamed two different dreams, on alternate nights. One was of Armageddon; the world was bombarded with flame, though I of course was the center of the bombardment, the peculiar and particular target. In the other I died and found myself in hell, a Christian and suffering more from simple astonishment in being there than from the enveloping flame. I gazed over the gulf into heaven's air-conditioned bliss only to see, double woe, the Buddhists sitting cozily in Abraham's bosom: *the Buddhists*, for Christ's sake, to whom we sent missionaries; I begged them to dip their fingers in the lake for a single drop to cool my parched tongue. I never had a dream about being in heaven.

I suspect it is not possible to convey the burden of Original Sin to anybody who hasn't been condemned to hell long before birth. The psychological condition of which Freud's punitive superego is a working metaphor gets close by analogy. The superego constantly monitors and controls an ego that desires to do something both instinctual and intrinsic to its survival *and* forbidden. Grounds for punishment are in place long before the ego can understand the very concept of "forbidden." Likewise, for Baptists, grounds for punishment, for self-laceration, exist long before consciousness, long before history even: In Adam's fall we sinned all. (Eve committed the first sin and then tempted Adam, who passed the sin on to the rest of us, so that even in sin men get the priority while women get the blame.) Because we are born short of the glory of God, we must go to hell if we are not saved, *even if we never actually commit a sin ourselves.* Thus in effect *being born* is the original sin for which we are condemned to hell. Perfection is of course impossible; but even if we were to live perfect lives, like Jesus, from the first minute of our own brief span, we would still be at fault because of Adam and Eve. We are thus born destined to be punished eternally for *their* sins unless we be born again, unless we accept Jesus' gift of salvation.

Baptists can never be *good enough,* even after we are saved, but Christ will of course save us nevertheless if we believe, because he is a loving son of a loving father. But in and of our selves we are still and always unworthy of salvation because of that *Original* sin, which Baptist theology accepts as a literal historical event; we are certainly unworthy of Jesus' agony and death upon the cross. The gift of salvation, the gift we cannot earn, then, does nothing to ennoble either giver or receiver because it is given on the basis of the explicit agreement that we are not, and can never ever be, worthy recipients of it.

Original Sin is a heavy load to bear. We are born insufficient—"*in sin*"—because of somebody else's disobedience. If we die in grace, that too has more to do with what somebody else has done than with anything we can do for ourselves. We are born responsible to eternity but we are not given the capacity to negotiate our own way through life and to it. The only options we have, spiritually speaking, are to accept or reject the free gift of grace that Jesus offers us: eternal life in heaven or the same in hell. As options go, this doesn't leave much room for maneuvering. But that is precisely the point: maneuverability, instability, works against Truth, which can only be something unchangeable. Heaven and Hell are the most imaginative monuments to stasis ever conceived, the greatest instruments of social control and political oppression ever created. One boggles, almost in admiration, at the resourcefulness that could conceive such. The eternal options leave little room for anything but obedience.

But at least Baptists have the options to accept or reject Christ's gift, options that folks in non-Christian lands—the Chinese, the Hindus, the Buddhists—do not: if Jesus is *The* Way, *The* Truth, and *The* Light, it is an inescapable conclusion that those folks, who have never heard the gospel or had the choice explained to them, are bound irrevocably toward hell, even if regrettably (too bad: you should have been born Baptist). That's why missions are incumbent upon us: Go ye therefore. Baptist deacons and pastors and Sunday school teachers can discuss the eternal burning of all the ignorant Chinese with a poise and equanimity that was not smug but even crowned with compassion and concern—it's *our* duty to get them the message: their souls are in *our* hands—and coolly deflect questions about the fairness of all this into the larger incomprehensible mysteries of God's universe: we'll understand it all by and by. What we must do now is just have faith, believe. Believe what? That God is just and merciful and loving. But where's the evidence? How does that work out for all those Chinese that we don't have the time or resources to get missionaries to? That's not for us to know: we can't ever understand God's ways.

Thus besides being born guilty of and condemned by somebody else's misbehavior and having no way to pay for our own sins, we must nevertheless also assume the additional burden of other people's souls. If *we* get to decide for ourselves whether to go to hell or not, how can they who've never even been given the options be sent to hell because of an accident of birth? And further, to push to the reductio ad absurdum, which we often did, what if we should discover other life in the solar system? Would Jesus' death two thousand years ago suffice for them too? Must we send Billy Graham to preach to them or would Jesus have to go there himself and undergo another crucifixion?* And

---

*As I write, in August 1996, the discovery of microbes on a Martian meteorite has given rise to these same questions among theologians (*Newsweek*, August 19). We were forty years in advance at First Baptist.

suppose a Hindu or a murderer got saved on a deathbed, like the thief on the cross? Would he have the *same* reward in heaven as we who had fought the good fight all our lives would have? Where was the justice in that?

We spent *hours* in youth discussion groups trying to hack our ways through such theological tangles and snags, easily the modern equivalents in seriousness and pointlessness of those medieval discussions about how many angels can dance on the head of a pin: of such matters were our intellectual lives composed. It's easy now, thirty and forty years later, to see how preposterous such discussions were; but I assure you they were burning questions at the First Baptist Church of Picayune, and discussed with much earnestness: my God, we wanted *answers*, we seekers after truth. Except by implication in the questions, nobody ever suggested how monstrous a God had been concocted for us all out of the aggression and political temporizing of the Old Testament, how racist and elitist that God was, or how much overtime he put in in the service of our cultural and political imperialism. It was simply a fact that God was just and loving; everything else was shaped and fitted to that core.

v.

What Baptist fundamentalism most insidiously does is rob you of a claim on your self. Every affect of fundamentalism springs from this theft. The Church constantly insists, in sermon and song, on the evils of ego, and on the virtues of denying your self except when devoting it to Others:

> Others, Lord, yes others,
> Let this my motto be.
> Help me to live for others,
> That I might live like thee.

•   •   •

Have thine own way, Lord, Have thine own way.*
Thou art the potter, I am the clay.
Mold me and make me after thy will,
While I am waiting, Yielded and still.

        • • •

Just as I am without one plea,
But that thy blood was shed for me.
And that thou bid'st me come to thee,
O lamb of God I come, I come.*

        • • •

Amazing Grace how sweet the sound
That saved a wretch like me.
I once was lost but now am found
Was blind but now I see.

        • • •

Jesus paid it all,
All to him I owe.
Sin had left a crimson stain,*
He washed it white as snow.

        • • •

"Man of Sorrows," what a name
For the Son of God who came*
Ruined Sinners to reclaim!
Hallelujah! what a Saviour!

Guilty, vile and helpless we:
Spotless Lamb of God was He:

----

*We often relieved the monotony of the hymn service by playing a little game that allowed us to place the phrase "between the sheets," after certain phrases. This is one example. I've marked others with asterisks.

"Full atonement!" can it be?
Hallelujah! what a Saviour!

• • •

Come, ye sinners, poor and needy,
Weak and wounded, sick and sore;
Jesus ready stands to save you,
Full of pity, love and power.

Come ye weary, heavy laden,
Lost and ruined by the fall;
If you tarry till you're better,
You will never come at all.*

Let not conscience make you linger,
Nor of fitness fondly dream;
All the fitness he requireth
Is to feel your need of him.

I will arise and go to Jesus,
He will embrace me in his arms,*
In the arms of my dear Saviour,
Oh, there are ten thousand charms.*

• • •

Would you live for Jesus and be always pure and good?
Would you walk with Him within the narrow road?
Would you have him bear your burden, carry all your load?
Let Him have his way with thee.*

His power can make you what you ought to be;
His blood can cleanse your heart and make you free;
His love can fill your soul and you will see
'Twas best for Him to have His way with thee.

• • •

When I survey the wondrous cross
On which the Prince of glory died
My richest gain I count but loss,
And pour contempt on all my pride.

Forbid it, Lord! that I should boast,
Save in the death of Christ my God:
All the vain things that charm me most,
I sacrifice them to His blood.

See, from His head, His hands, His feet,
Sorrow and love flow mingled down:
Did e'er such love and sorrow meet,
Or thorns compose so rich a crown.

Were the whole realm of nature mine,
That were a present far too small;
Love so amazing, so divine,
Demands my soul, my life, my all.

Baptist theology and practice thus rob you of self; they leave you without form, void where a self might have been. More, they provide you nothing, no primal mud even, to create a self with, not even for traction to move about in. They give you no model of self to work toward, since the ideal self is a negation, a void you can fill only with Jesus, who is himself the crucified and suffering martyred embodiment of that ideal.

Baptist theology robs you of the pleasures of spontaneity by making you unrelentingly aware of *consequence*, of the possible disastrous end results of everything you might ever do, even of those things you might do inadvertently. It makes you so fearful of possibility—of freedom— that you simply shut down the spontaneous. This may be why Southern

Baptists, and southerners in general, are so fearful of change, not to say of revelry. Because we are of the Truth, we also have a responsibility not to be a stumbling block to others: others thus become a sort of Big Brother who constantly monitors us, watching to judge whether our deeds match our language. Jeremy Bentham with his panopticon and the Soviet Union's oligarchy with all their apparatus were bumbling amateurs, clumsy voyeurs compared to the totality of the organization with which the Baptist church keeps you in line with your own selfconsciousness; it controls you by watching you even through the eyes of nonbelievers, the very sinners you are supposed to influence and whom, of course, you cannot influence if your life is no different from theirs.

It's hardly accurate to say that I was "scarred" by religion, since scars result from healing, and since scars locate separate sites on a body or spirit where injury has been inflicted by some agency different from and external to it. "Wound" and "scar" are the wrong metaphors, though they are so dear and even essential to Baptists. The kind of pounding that Simon McEachern gives Joe Christmas in Faulkner's *Light in August*, so often accepted as a *sine qua non* of the repressive puritan spirit in action, is not even a useful metaphor for the kind of spiritual injury I want to describe. The horror of Baptist actuality is that you don't know you are in pain; it is as though you are born with a migraine headache as a given of your existence, internal, intimate, essential: you don't even experience it as pain because you've never experienced painlessness. Baptists don't beat you into submission, then; it's hardly ever necessary, since you've already submitted, as to breathing, long before consciousness.

To be healed requires first of all that you realize that you have been breathing poison. To be healed requires that you recognize that your condition in sin is not a natural condition but rather an affect of the church's control of all your epistemological systems. To be healed requires that you destroy a system that has been, is, essential to your very existence.

I don't mean that proximate, visible, articulated system that upholds the Father, Son, and Holy Ghost, that offers Christ's wounds as the only sufficiency for your condition "in sin": *that* system is easy enough to deal with, to believe or not believe. I mean rather that other, that implicit and unarticulated one that operates invisibly, the necessary dark underbelly to the Triune God, that remains in place long after you have become Episcopalian or agnostic or atheist. It is more like a virus, which pervades and dominates your body's psychic systems, mostly lying dormant but which even when you are in remission can still, under certain stimuli, irrupt in a spiritual suppuration that marks you painfully.

If you're lucky you wake up one day when you are middleaged and you discover just how insidious the ideal of selflessness is. But the discovery brings with it a terrifying ideological dislocation and the necessity to restructure the ideological bases of your life, which fundamentalists, clinging to Truth, resist. When your belief systems crumble, you find yourself struggling to breathe something besides poison—as the person who wakes up one morning without the migraine he or she has had from birth can experience painlessness only as pain because the lack of pain is the deviation from the normal, from the True. You discover that you can actually live your life on your own terms, can actually think that "selfishness" does not have to be morally problematic. You discover this in your head but your every instinct is honed from years of habit to resist thinking this way, or at least to resist acting on it without much soul-wrenching. To act requires a deliberate, calculated assertion of a self that you are still trying to locate, or create, after so many years of self-abnegation.

The idea of having your own life, of catering to your own needs, even of simply treating your own needs as equal in value with those of others, is as alien and seems as unattainable as the concept of red is to the colorblind. Even intellectually free of the notion that selfishness is immoral you are not morally or psychologically free from your obsession with consequence, and so you spend endless hours calibrating where your right to a life begins and your children's, say, ends: what legitimate claims do they have on you and how do their legitimate claims impinge on your own rights to a life of your own? What happens—today, tomorrow—if you decide to indulge yourself? These are conflicts that Baptists resolve by simply dismissing them: selfishness is sin, devotion to others a virtue. Baptists, like Dostoevski's Grand Inquisitor, know that freedom is, for most people, an intolerable condition. Thus selflessness is a recognition of the church community's claim on you, a self-divestiture of individual freedom.

But selflessness is in fact the debilitating contradiction at the heart of Baptist Christianity, a problem much less easy to theologize away than the old chestnut paradox of God's intervention in history, the divine nose-snubbing at time which allowed the Word to be made flesh, the abstract to become concrete. Given one hundred percent— millions—of individual, free, assertable selves, fundamentalism would collapse, as would any ideology of social control, including patriotism and nationalism: what we are willing to give up of desire is what makes social cohesion possible. Baptists, then, who value order and control— Truth—above all, do not, cannot, allow you to think of your own claims on your own life, your claims on your own needs. Nowhere do church leaders show more brilliance or practicality—or cynicism—than in this: they do some fancy footwork around the problem and instead use it to create the structure that makes Christianity, the church anyway, possible.

If *everybody* practiced it, selflessness would create vacuum, implode and drag the rest of the world in to the black hole it would create. Someone must assume responsibility, someone must decide, someone must assert, someone must lead; there must be some, even among the saints, who don't give up self completely so that there can be some organizing center, principle, for those who do. Those who do give up self thus become vulnerable to those who don't; they come to depend entirely on Saviours and their earthly avatars, political and military and even romantic. Looking for somebody to feed, the docile selfless wait for somebody to feed them too; looking for somebody to sacrifice themselves for, they readily yield themselves to those willing to be sacrificed to. They are ripe for exploitation. Hence the Crusades, hence the military popes, hence the battlecry of God and Country, hence the millions who have been massacred or enchained in the name of one God or cause or another, hence wives and children who are battered and abused. All political structures, including the church and the family, assume that some dominate, others be dominated. Christianity thus forestalls the vacuum and chaos that its own theology would inevitably cause by creating hierarchy, and hierarchy creates victims—actual victims or simply the mindless followers of the system who allow the abuse, the repression, to happen in their names.

If I had been a Roman official or a Jewish leader, upon hearing the Sermon on the Mount, especially the Beatitudes, I would not only *not* have crucified Jesus, I would have rented the Galilean equivalent of a flatbed truck, put a podium on it all decked out in flags and state seals, and personally driven him around the countryside to every Judaean village and town, supplying him with microphones or megaphones or whatever it would take to get that message across to the locals. I'd have made him the televangelist equivalent of his day (if I were a showbiz entrepreneur, I'd want to be his agent), so long as he continued to preach such exhortations to meekness, to passivity, to keeping God and Caesar separate while of course rendering to both and rendering in ways that don't disturb the temporal status quo. But the Romans and Jews knew better: they knew that the best way to broadcast and preserve the message was to identify it as subversive, to brand the preacher a political criminal, and to make of him a martyr. Thus they continued their political control over the masses by allowing them to invest their submission with divine sanction. Render unto Caesar indeed.

There is no more persuasive articulation of the virtues of passivity than the Beatitudes: each apothegm is a carefully crafted assault on the self, a calculated admonition to precisely the sort of selflessness that gives the individual no claim on a life of her or his own—at least a life in this world: we can claim our lives only in the next. Jesus was thus not only not a political troublemaker, he actually enjoined folks not to resist Caesar at all but to render unto him; he did not separate God and Caesar but actually forced their inextricability. This doesn't sound very revolutionary to me:

> Blessed are the poor in spirit: for theirs is the kingdom of heaven. Blessed are they that mourn: for they shall be comforted. Blessed are the meek: for they shall inherit the earth. Blessed are they which do hunger and thirst after righteousness: for they shall be filled. Blessed are the merciful: for they shall obtain mercy. Blessed are the pure in heart: for they shall see God. Blessed are the peacemakers: for they shall be called the children of God. Blessed are they which are persecuted for righteousness' sake: for theirs is the kingdom of heaven. Blessed are ye, when men shall revile you, and persecute you, and shall say all manner of evil against you falsely, for my sake. Rejoice, and be exceeding glad: for great is your reward in heaven: for so persecuted they the prophets which were before you. (Matthew 5:3–12)

These are fine sentiments if you are a Have: fine, that is, for all Have-nots—for the poor in spirit, the mourners, the meek, the merciful—to believe, because it is to a Have's advantage for Have-nots to forego aggression and desire, to be content with their lot. That's why fundamentalist Christianity is essentially nihilistic: it insists that you focus on rewards in a highly problematic other life rather than on getting what you want or can have in this one. The biblical rhetoric, to be sure, teaches that we must give in order to receive, give up in order to have; that's the kind of paradox fundamentalists can deal with because giving up, denial, is so easy: in a material sense it is easy to deny yourself things you aren't likely to get anyway. If you argue to a Baptist that Christianity is nihilistic, you are likely to be met with a smile and a gentle reminder that Jesus said "I am come that ye might have life and have it more abundantly." But his "abundance" means spiritual plenty, not material. Indeed, the Beatitudes teach you to be happy and content with nothing, which is both what you have and the most you can expect on this earth, and it's why you invest so desperately in a heavenly reward. The Beatitudes give hope—the best, and the worst, of gifts. People can have all of hope they want, and are encouraged for hope to be enough for the time being. Hope is more essential than bread: people will go hungry for the sake of hope, they will kill and maim and die for it. And so who supplies hope controls everything.

The injunction to render unto Caesar is absolute, it carries no qualification: it does not enjoin us to negotiate, to render so long as Caesar renders appropriately or equally back to us in fair exchange: goods, services, security, retirement pensions. Happiness, then—salvation—comes from lowered expectations: when you have hope you don't have to deal with desire. Happiness comes from docility, from not expecting, much less demanding, anything of Caesar in return. Render to Caesar and to God: yield yourself always to authority, no matter how authority is constituted. Thus for the fundamentalist God and Country, Jesus and Patriotism, are forever twinned, wedded, inextricable.

It is no wonder, then, that Christianity's two basic tropes are sheep and soldiers, two seemingly contradictory characteristics, except for what soldiers and sheep have in common, the quality of unquestioning obedience to whoever, whatever, is out in front—leading to their own slaughter or to someone else's. Fundamentalists are indeed easily manipulated by theogogues who provide them with hope and purpose through the rhetoric of God and freedom. Life is a battle we as sheep are not suited to fight, so we must also be soldiers constantly girding our loins with the breastplates of righteousness (as I heard one preacher put it) and accepting the shepherd's implicit instruction that we can win in this struggle only if we do what somebody else tells us, even if that means sacrificing ourselves or, most regrettably, attacking and murdering other people and cultures. Life for Baptists is a constant struggle, a serious serious business. Internally it is a struggle with eternity, with doubt, externally a political and social struggle with a variety of foes (desire, communism, change) whose existence somehow challenges and threatens even an Allpowerful God, and whose defeat will certify the "rightness" of our cause.

Two sermons I have never heard in any church are on Bible passages most troublesome to institutional structure. The first is Jesus' quite extraordinary and politically revolutionary claim, "You shall know the truth and the truth shall make you free." Actually, I have heard this passage quoted approvingly from the pulpit, but its real, scintillating, and quite fearful message gets watered down in the semantics of freedom, with discussions of the difference between freedom and license. Even literalist readers of the Bible find it necessary to "interpret" such outrageous statements: we have to understand what "freedom" means.

"Oh: it doesn't just mean *freedom*?"

"Well, yes, but he's talking about a higher freedom that you can only attain to if you trust in him."

"Oh. So you submit in order to be free?"

"Right."

"But how can you be free if you submit?"

"You have to be a Christian to understand: Jesus also said that you have to give up life in order to have it."

"Oh. I see. No: I don't see."

"It's very simple if you believe."

"Believe? How can you believe you're free if you're not free?"

"You have to understand what he meant by freedom."

"He didn't just mean freedom is freedom?"

"He did, but you have to understand—"

Doubtless they are right, actually: the man who articulated the Beatitudes is not one who believes in any form of freedom as commonly understood.

The other passage is even more problematic, though it is related, since it carries us right back to the scene of the Original Crime, the Garden of Eden, where all of our troubles started. But it gives a considerably different slant on what the troubles are and on who caused them:

> And the Lord God said, Behold, the man is become as one of us, to know good and evil: and now, lest he put forth his hand, and take also of the tree of life, and eat, and live forever: Therefore the Lord God sent him forth from the garden of Eden, to till the ground from whence he was taken. So he drove out the man; and he placed at the east of the garden of Eden Cherubims, and a flaming sword which turned every way, to keep the way of the tree of life. (Genesis 3:22–24)

There is thus a second forbidden tree in the garden but you'd never know it from listening to Baptist sermons (how other denominations deal with that second tree I am not completely sure, but I recently tried talking about it to a group of Episcopalians and got nowhere). Sermons always talk about that other tree, the tree of the knowledge of good and evil, the site of Eve's and Adam's easily explicable disobedience of God's law. Discussions of that tree assume God's law, his forbidding of the fruit, as reasonable, or at least as something not to be questioned. The passage about the tree of life, however, suggests that there's a good deal questionable about God's law; it therefore provides plenty of *scriptural* reason to question the biblical God's relationship with and attitude toward human beings.

The passage about the second tree, the tree of life, is precisely about the arbitrariness of God's power; the reason for the prohibitions against eating the fruit of the other tree can only be to assert and maintain that power. God's power therefore must be vulnerable to attack, as Adam and Eve demonstrate in their disobedience. But the reason God expels them from the garden is *not* their disobedience, as the sermonic tradition would have it, but rather, quite to the contrary, the fact that God *feared* the challenge their disobedience poses. Thus he admits that he is not omnipotent: knowing good and evil they might become "as one" of the several gods. The second tree, then, points to several questions that sermons completely beg: why prohibitions in Eden in the first place, except as an arbitrary marker of power? Why would an omnipotent God need to mark his power? It would seem petty and tyrannical, not to say paranoid and insecure, for an omnipotent God, one who had created the universe in six days, to worry overmuch about the antics of two of his own creations. Obviously, then, he didn't want to share power. The only way not to share power is to exercise it. So freedom is not and can never be part of a Baptist's arsenal, no matter how much the literalists argue that the only true freedom is the freedom to love God—and obey. The most generous interpretation of the passage is that God very well understood that freedom would have terrified humanity and that he built prohibition into the system precisely for that reason; that's actually an interpretation one might live with, but I'm not sure it gives us a more attractive God than the one who prohibits arbitrarily: why did he not create us not to be fearful of freedom?

There are understandable and predictable parallels to this second tree in the way that morality gets transmitted and taught in the Baptist system, a system that equates freedom with disobedience. Since the essence of sin is disobedience, it follows that freedom and sin are identical too, and can only lead to disaster. The rhetoric from church leaders to young people is entirely of prohibition: don't. Usually, the prohibition is a simplistic reduction of morality to the two cardinal concerns of Southern Baptist morality, alcohol and sex; the prohibition in practice usually divides responsibility between the sexes, so that the underlying message of the prohibition, whatever its actual language, is "Boys: don't drink. Girls: don't be sexual." The prohibition thus assigns to women the responsibility for everybody's sexual behavior; naturally, boys get off the sexual hook, though the prohibition against drinking is a mild cautionary against losing control: at least help the girls maintain responsibility for your sexual life. I report this from my memories at Picayune First Baptist of years ago and from more recent experience in Hattiesburg; I can only assume that the intervening forty years have not been much different.

I have never heard in a Baptist church any discussion of morality that did not begin and end with "Don't." No pastor or youth director or evangelist either, in my hearing, made any effort to talk about choice, about personal responsibility. They assumed in fact that, given the legitimate choice to have sex or not to have it, girls, frail vessels of temptation that they are, would naturally choose to have it. Though Baptists constantly admonish young women against yielding to social pressures, they almost completely deny such other realities as a need for love created by dysfunction at home and other situations in which females are victimized, including rape and incest, that force women to be sexual whether they want to or not.

I never heard one single Baptist leader try to give young women a sense of self sufficient to allow them to be able to say no just because they choose to, to say no with freedom and dignity rather than from fear; for Baptists they must say no because they *must* say no, and for no other reason. Young women who experiment with sex just because they like it do so most guiltily, since the system abhors pleasure above all; those who are sexually active for the wrong reasons—because they think sex is the only way they can get some attention or the love they are not getting at home—are thus reassured only that they are as wicked as they have been taught to believe they naturally are. The church thus cuts them off from any of the kinds of help that might in fact empower them to make moral choices, to choose how they will conduct their lives. Church leaders are of course right: given the choice, some will say yes, and that's the fear, the entire problem with freedom: some will make choices that they shouldn't make, choices that will lead to disastrous consequences.

The prohibitions often come from the tenders of the second tree who, I have certain knowledge, were themselves often rambunctious as teenagers, who even as they prohibit their children are themselves engaged in various activities, sexual and otherwise, that the church would not approve of. They have made it through their own teen years unscathed and now, to put the best light on it, are afraid their children won't be as lucky as they were; to put the worst light on it, they don't want their children to taste the forbidden fruit of freedom, don't want their children to become as they are. More recently, I have known one woman who, being honest with her Sunday school class of teen girls, confessed that she had not been so lucky as a teen: she had gotten pregnant, then badly married, then divorced. She offered her own life as a cautionary tale about the bad things that can happen when freedom is not careful with itself. Instead of accolades for her honesty, for her practical wisdom, the church, an otherwise comparatively liberal one, roundly, though not publicly, condemned her.

Whatever the rhetoric of the theology, then, it is not a rhetoric of morality; quite the contrary, since morality is an active engagement with choice. The prohibition forefends the knowledge of good and evil precisely by forbidding choice. At its best, its most compassionate, Baptist theology works to keep us in an Edenic state of innocence, to keep us safe; but that is also Baptist theology at its worst, since innocence is a state inimical to morality and a denial of the basic premises of the condition Christ died to save us from.

The other constant Baptist admonition to teenagers is to Obey Your Parents. This admonition, because biblical, is also absolute and unqualified. It makes no exceptions for children who are dispirited and confused because they are caught between this admonition on the one hand and abusive or indifferent parents on the other, and so the only possible conclusion they can come to is that they themselves are somehow to blame for their misery: *something is wrong with me; something is going to happen to me.* The church thus confirms abusive families in their power over helpless suffering children; the church and the family and the state hold each others' hands in a tight network of intricately related systems that keep the individual captive. They are primarily concerned with their own preservation, at no matter what cost to the individuals within the system. Religion, like politics, is finally about power; obviously freedom has no place in the Baptist mentality.

Given what we now know about the kind of abuse that goes on in the American family it may be possible to account for American conservative resistance to such putative "socialist" ideas as public day-care centers: who to know, parents have doubtless feared, what kinds of things children might tell if they were gathered together in a clean well-lighted place run by professionals?

v i .

The experience of being "saved" is as impossible to describe as the burden of Original Sin. Though fundamentalists will discuss the metaphorical nature of being "born again," there is in fact a debilitating literalness about the need for new Christians to become "as a little child": "Except ye be converted and become as little children, ye shall not enter into the kingdom of heaven" (Matthew 18:3). It's a perfect complement to the problematics of choice.

What do we need salvation *from?* The popular notion is that Baptists scare you into salvation with threats of hellfire, and to be sure there are a gracious plenty of sermons, tracts, and other exhortations that sell salvation as a form of fire insurance. But that is not really what necessitates salvation. For all my adolescent worry about eternity in hell, my own "salvation" had little or nothing to do with heaven or hell; that worry came later, post-salvation, when doubt set in. What we seek salvation from is precisely, and merely, the emptiness, the loneliness, at the core of the human experience.

The need to be saved is a response to that loneliness, which is a condition of human life. Baptists, however, define that condition not as loneliness but as a condition of loss into which we are born—a loss of something we can find if we know where to look. Thus the story of salvation is a story told backwards, like history, to explain an existing condition, to locate its cause in a preexisting structure from which we have defected not by choosing to defect but by being born. For Baptists, it is not simply a condition in loneliness but a condition of alienation from God created by our inheritance of Adam's and Eve's disobedience, and so a condition in sin. It is therefore a condition created by the system that also simultaneously supplies the salvation from it: the one is created by the other, they both exist intra-dependently, one could not exist without the other. They both exist, according to the Bible, not because of disobedience in the Garden of Eden but because of God's jealousy of human possibilities in freedom.

Freedom from time and space, then, is the defining characteristic of God, and so he had to get Adam and Eve out of the Garden because otherwise, having discovered the knowledge of good and evil, they would eventually discover the full implications of their act of disobedience; they would understand that their condition was not at all in sin but rather in freedom; not a condition of loss but a condition of possibility. In fact, then, Adam and Eve didn't discover the knowledge of good and evil at all: they rather discovered submission; their core story discovers to us how hierarchy constructs good and evil as tools to condemn whatever opposes it. Their expulsion from the Garden taught them that disobedience was bad; God gave them no reason to think it was good, which is precisely the point. Of course, Baptists teach the curious and paradoxical concept of the fortunate fall, which is, under the circumstances, a fallback position. Only by our fall could we have learned what good is; only through our disobedience could Christ's love have been made manifest in the world. This position is all the more outrageous and frustrating since God of course precipitated the fall by being vulnerable to dispossession in the first place. The exercise of freedom is what got us kicked out of the Garden, what put us in need of salvation.

Salvation means yielding to structures of community and hierarchy that our human condition as selves, not to say our moral condition as choosers, alienates us from: salvation means letting go of whatever remnants of self remain. The rhetoric identifies those remnants as pride, selfishness, egotism, intellectualism, and vanity; it argues that only by relinquishing our life can we find it, only by sinking our selves into a larger community can we find relief from our unrelievable freedom, from the inviolably private places where we confront, always alone, the great questions of eternity. These are, of course, questions the church itself has imposed on us; and, constantly flexing its ideological muscle, it forces us to respond to its questions in the terms of its answers. Its questions and its answers are a locked grid in which we have to function. For one brought up in the tradition, it is a major step to understand that there might be other answers, not to say other questions. People are afraid of freedom and will do almost anything to escape it. And so salvation means yielding to the preexisting conditions that both the preexisting questions and the preexisting answers confirm; it means yielding to the community that has set the agenda, becoming part of the handholding fellowship that gathers around the cross to worship the crucified Savior.

I can testify that yielding is relief: for a few moments, a few days, for some maybe a lifetime, you quit striving with your inexorable, demanding self and allow it to be swallowed up, as Jonathan Edwards put it, into something greater and more magnificent, even if not more comprehensible, than your worthless self. For a time you are absolved into the community of folks who embrace you in their collective yielding, and for a time you feel indeed purified, "born again," relieved of aloneness, of freedom. But "born again" is precisely the wrong metaphor, it's just exactly backward: *wombed again* is more apt, since "born again" would mean emerging from the security-womb your church and your culture happily provide you, if you can just accept them and stop thinking about it. But to be re-wombed, I say, to yield, is wonderful. For a time it is like flying: you are absolutely, astonishingly liberated from time, body, mind, worry: for a time it is like soaring, frictionless, through alpine heights or around the moon: a rush and roar of exhilaration, a release of tears and hilarity, an ecstasy.

For a time. And then it is just falling: the old weights and measures, the minute qualifications, the checks, the doubts, the immutable selfishness of desire assert themselves, at first like bubbles rising from a sour swamp; then, the swamp itself rising, your soar becomes a swim in a bog. Your asserting need confronts all the admonitions to selflessness you have been taught; it troubles you into fearfulness, into doubt, and you move again down and around from intensity to despair, until you again feel lost lost lost, and all the more confused because you know that you have been saved, or rather thought you had but obviously have not because if you had been how could you possibly be experiencing this much anxiety? Visions of hell assault you nightly and you have no way out but to try the same route in again. Hence another popular altar call at the end of Baptist sermons was for "re-dedication." Folks came forward who felt that though they were Christians they had not been leading the right kind of life and so were lacking the joy in their salvation that was their right. Revivals often saw "re-deds" by the dozen.

Given our sheep-soldier mentality, it is not difficult to understand how easily Baptists, fundamentalists, are mobilized into conservative political action, how readily we spout the jargon that claims a hold on Truth that is utterly without basis in experience or history, how easily we are convinced, at the extreme, that we need to "defend" our values from attack by infidels, even if such defenses mean dying ourselves or killing somebody else.

My bleakest reflections on these things lead to dark conclusions about humanity's capacity or even desire to exercise the kinds of political and moral freedoms that would see right and wrong not as moral absolutes handed down from above to a chosen people but rather as practical considerations in a constant negotiation of power between and among different constituencies. Darkly put, people do not want and they cannot survive in the vacuum, the isolation, of political and moral freedom; we are all Baptists in clinging to certainty, especially when moral certainty can be aligned with nationalism or regionalism. Without some ideological structure to cohere around, most peoples would dissolve in chaos; we are eager to be led, to be lied to, so long as we can keep our ideological structures firmly in place: we'd rather die than give up or question our illusions. This fact constitutes the absolute bind of people in power, whether secular or religious: the unillusioned powerful know how important illusions are to any social or political group. Politicians know how easily people can be led and manipulated by their illusions, which they would call their ideals. The unillusioned, like the Grand Inquisitor, know that nations must be fed a diet equally of ideology as of bread, or even cake.

It is easy to ridicule and caricature those relatively few Baptists whose excrescences of faith, whose meanspirited, repressive politics and moral-ity form the basis of the religious hypocrite and cripple of the southern stereotype: but they are too simple a target. In some ways they are to be both pitied, for we know their pathologies, and feared, since in these days many have attained to a certain destructive influence. But they inspire in survivors neither pity nor fear but only a faint sense of the ominous—that cobra again—at the workings of a faith that allows and even encourages the Old Doc Hineses and the Simon McEacherns and their televangelical brethren. It is far easier to patronize, even with contempt, the sheep mentality that produces the congregations that follow Jimmy Jones to Guyana or even those that simply accept, without question, a faith that forces them to follow whoever is leading, wherever he is going, especially if he is leading down the path of tradition, which is the path of stasis.

Though our racial attitudes were politically of their time and place, we at First Baptist, Picayune, in the fifties thought of ourselves as essentially apolitical, and even used the church's claim to serve spiritual rather than temporal needs as our reason for staying out of the politics of racial justice (except, of course, to maintain the status quo. Barely a year or so ago, Southern Baptists officially apologized for slavery; but I've not seen much evidence of any effort to do much more than that). I do not know what First Baptist, Picayune's political stance is now, when televangelists have ratcheted up the church's spiritual agenda into a shrilly political one. I do not know whether those good people of the fifties or their descendants have changed with the political times, whether they are as overtly intolerant and fearful as their denomination in general has recently become.

Yet it would be wrong to ridicule or patronize the members of First Baptist during my time in Picayune, and no less wrong to ridicule or patronize other individual Baptists and fundamentalists at any time. The folks at Picayune, as I say, were mostly dear, sweet, loving people who wouldn't have followed Jimmy Jones even to Guyana, much less to the grave, and I rather suspect that most members there then would not have sent money to support Jim Bakker's looniness or Pat Robertson's political agenda ("Televise the Second Coming *my hind foot!*" Georgia Jones would have said.) but would rather have given it locally for home or foreign mission programs; perhaps they occasionally sent a love offering to Billy Graham, both fervent and respectable.

*   *   *

The wonder—the paradox, actually, given the way I've presented things here—is not in how many Baptists escape the meanspiritedness and self-righteousness that characterizes so many prominent fundamentalists—certainly those of the Baptist myth—but rather in fact that so many do seem to find in the homilies, in the Beatitudes, in the example of the self-sacrificial Christ, a standard for living that actually gives them that peace that passeth understanding, a standard that manifests itself as a generally charitable agenda of medical and social aid to afflicted peoples (along with a gospel lesson, of course), and a genuine concern for others.

I do *of course* understand that the concern for "others" is too often a concern for the other-who-is-like-myself or who is at a distance only missionaries can travel, and that "others" who have different skin colors or national origins and who live locally are more likely to be political and social irritants than those distant "others" to whom we are adjured to sacrifice ourselves. Sacrifice has its limits, even for Baptists. I understand how such communal selflessness operates to exclude rather than include, how it works to keep all likes attracted to the like at the center, magnetized to it and to each other, a clotting of folks crowding to the center, trying to annihilate themselves at and in the center itself. But this crowding toward the center is tribal, by no means exclusive to Baptists.

And yet, within that exclusionary company manners predominate: there is very little pushing and shoving at the center, a good deal of holding the door for others, and not just for the elderly or disabled. Within that exclusionary company there indeed does operate a sweetness of spirit, a gentleness, a humility, that tries to put into practice all that we have been taught are the genuine Christian virtues. Perhaps after all the belief in Grace creates its daily reality, parsed out in separate moments of grace given and received; perhaps that is the most anyone can expect—and by no means a bad thing.

I expect that Picayune Baptists did not, do not, pursue the church's theological systems so relentlessly as I have here. They seemed to have found contentment with the larger picture, the one that made them secure, happy with their place in a system that allows, encourages, simple manners to control the quotidian concreteness of their lives.

But what the system seems to have given them, comfort and peace, it denied to many of its Baptist sons and daughters, even those who tried their damnedest to find a secure place in it for themselves and couldn't, because the system has no place for negotiation, for anybody with a question that hasn't already been answered a billion times since 2,000 years ago. It is no purpose of mine to question any individual's faith, or to unsettle what has been settled. But I do wonder whether a faith that exists in a historical vacuum—that has never questioned itself, that has not been freely chosen from among thousands of possibilities but merely accepted as handed down—has not purchased security and peace at the exorbitant price of freedom, of personal responsibility, and does not lend itself to the political expedience of those who would use it to their own ends. That's perhaps why it's disquieting to survivors to know how many thousands live and die within that growing Baptist bosom, believe in their destinies and in their missions and, above all, seem sweetly content, joyous even.

Even so, the habit of those early years makes some form of belief attractive for survivors, even in our unillusion. Survivors often long for a posture of worship that is no longer available to us. We might even like to become that little child that Jesus invests with wisdom, to be uncritical, unthinking, accepting; but, alas, we live our lives as adults. The peace that passeth understanding is, with understanding, what we have perforce given up.

That early habit promotes the lingering affection for the hymns and the fellowship, and it would like to find somewhere some niche for such as we who whether we believe in God or not at least believe in Mystery and like peoples from the beginning of time would like to find some forum, if not an altar, to which we might bring both our belief and our unbelief, where we might touch base with other negotiators: it's why we read and think, after all. But Baptists operate in absolutes, not in shades or complexities, and so we negotiators have no place in the Baptist system, perhaps not in any system. It's just as well. What we find when we look behind Baptist doors today is the same old sweet death we have run from for all these years.

v i i .

God's original plan would have precluded history. We would have existed in a comfortably static Eden, free of desire and time. Freud observes, correctly, that there are no prohibitions against things nobody wants to do. But prohibition creates the desire to do the thing prohibited: thus God created desire, and therefore time, by imposing prohibition. At the fall, God instituted Plan B, which would allow the human race to be redeemed from time, desire, and rebelliousness through faith in his son's blood sacrifice. According to Plan B, Jesus, outside of time himself, would enter it, suffer and die for our disobedience in having entered time ourselves, reign in heaven and then return to earth to abolish his (our) enemies and to gather the faithful to him in paradise—a paradise curiously not that original rural Eden, but a more urban one, with gold-paved streets, mansions for all to inhabit, and other citified amenities.

For Baptists, then, history is, or should be, anathema, for it is by definition a record of, an admission of, change, a denial of and challenge to the one true and unchanging Eternal Reality that for us stands outside of time. History for Baptists records humanity's rebellious deviation from Plan A, Christ's intervention into that deviation, and Christianity's subsequent efforts to redirect the human chronicle, by main force or whatever force is available, back into concord with the original plan.

A good deal of southern meditation on our history and culture springs from the inexplicable, and not completely articulated, discrepancy between the demonstrable problems in our economy and our social institutions and the moral superiority we more often claim than demonstrate. We are a stable society, we claim; we love God, we love Nature, even if we prefer to live in the city; we love family and country: we have the right *values*. So how could God let the unGodly North humiliate us so? It would be reasonable, you'd think, to admit that we must not have been "right" in our institutions and attitudes, and so rethink our commitments to the "way of life" that caused the problem in the first place. But southern and Baptist honor is completely invested in being right, in holding on to Truth, whatever the cost. We are a moral and beautiful and interesting and significant people, no matter what our history.

At the center of southern and Baptist spiritual and political life, then, is, appropriately, the crucified Christ—icon relic and totem of our self-effacement. How better to symbolize our history as southerners and Baptists, the lifetime of condescension, the slights and the defeats our selflessness has invited upon us? We lift him up and he provides us eternal vengeance of a peculiar and pathological sort: broken, bleeding, loving those who love him but loving also those who hate him, saving the dying thief, doing good to the very last, under the most trying of circumstances—dying for the right, crucified by an infidel world.

Lifted up, he draws us to him. He draws us by appropriating us, and we are eager to be appropriated. He is a mirror in which we see our own broken self, a self that we believe ourselves to be: blameless, gentle, loved, presiding eternally, serenely, over our enemies from the superiority of our cross: victorious in our very defeat, justified finally in our suffering. For Baptists, martyrdom is the best thing of all. We cling to it, irreconcilable. It's the truth of our history. It's how we can get beaten and still be right. It's how, lost, we find ourselves.

Touching Base

A week before Thanksgiving 1992 my Uncle Alton learned that he was going to die, before Christmas, of the same cancer his sister Virgie had died of forty years before. My Aunt Virginia, his youngest sister, called to tell me—or, rather, she had gotten her son Farley, my cousin, to call me, perhaps to save a long-distance call since he and I live in Hattiesburg. Though we lived barely fifty miles from each other, I had not seen Alton, or many of my other relatives, since my father's funeral in 1968. There's no particular reason for our not visiting. We had just fallen into the sort of disuse families fall into when there is no powerful center, like my father, to cohere around, and after his death we had all refracted and retrenched into our own separate circles. We had not extended ourselves like the traditional family of southern fabrication, but instead moved, sometimes tentatively, in our own ellipsoid orbits around Picayune, where we had lived, and which we all have continued to call home no matter how far removed we were, geographically or otherwise. I'm not even sure that my children, now grown, ever met Alton.

Monday before Thanksgiving Mother and I went to see Alton at Caesar, his home just outside of Picayune, a pine-swaddled community of Lees and Shaws and Ladners, many of whom I am related to in one legal or blood connection or another. There we met Durscherl, Alton's wife; Virginia, who lives in Gulfport, about 60 miles from Caesar; my Uncle Austin, all the way from Texas; and Farley. It was a reunion: we took up as if there had been no gap at all. We sat and visited, as amicably as ever, with him who was to die, talking of his death just as we might talk, did talk, of the changing weather, a new automobile. Alton sat in a sort of easy chair in the living room, facing the front door and so turned away from the end of the narrowish room where the sofas were and where by ordinary we all could have sat comfortably while we visited. The others sat in a little circle around him in kitchen chairs arranged for the moment; assuming we'd sit on the sofas, I had deposited myself there, and so sat outside the circle; I mostly saw Alton's animated profile as we talked, though he constantly turned his head to include me. While we talked he ate a huge dinner of fried catfish, brought to him by my cousin Ray, Virgie's son, from the catfish restaurant just down the road owned by Ray's brother Jerry and his family.

Alton's eyes as he talked were as bright and mischievous as ever, and he affected the same verbal swagger, ran through the same repertoire of very bad jokes that had been his staples since my very earliest memories of him, the ones that families use to nag and threaten and accuse in good fun: "Well, Noel, you ain't got any better looking since I saw you last," he said when we got there, looking me up and down with short, rapid glances, and grinning; "You don't behave while you're here I'm gonna get outa this chair and take you on. I can still do it." He talked with a barely suppressed glee which might any minute, and frequently did, break out in a giggle.

Virginia had told me that he had been moving in and out of consciousness, had been having long remarkable conversations with my father, so I was more or less prepared when he flashed his eyes and reported on those conversations, with my father, with Virgie, his parents—all in heaven, all happily awaiting him, he said. "I know *you* don't believe this," he said, turning and twinkling in my direction; he doubtless knew he was right but accepted that and talked in that constant teasing swagger of his, putting me on, as he always did about everything else, both allowing me and daring me not to believe him. "But your daddy"—yo *dad*dy, he pronounced it—"loves you and says tell you you better behave," he said.

"What part don't I believe, your Ugliness?" I said. "That he loves me or that you talked to him?" He giggled.

"Are they all happy?" Austin wanted to know.

"Oh, yeah," Alton said, striking a beatific pose like those old cheap Sunday school portraits of Jesus, and I swear he glowed; maybe it was anticipation, maybe the brightness of the teeth inside his grin, maybe just my pleasure in connecting again.

"What's it like there?" I asked, wanting to keep him going, and as fascinated by the whole scene as by anything I'd observed in a long time. I had come dreading this visit, expecting to find a grim fearful reunion with one I hardly knew anymore and could expect never to see again and found myself instead at instant ease in the old comfortable grooves of our mutual lives, long gone in neglect.

"It's so wonderful," he said, and ran his hands up and down his legs, his trunk, his cancer-eaten body. "So much better than here."

When he got tired Durscherl put him to bed. We left, one by one, after a final and private goodbye. I sat down on his bed, leaned over, and we hugged; he grappled me hard, like a bear. I was surprised at his strength.

"Tell Papa it's o.k.," I said.

I could feel his unshaven face, his broad wet smile working against my cheek. "He told me you'd say that. I love you, Noel," he said, and I wept too, for loss, for love.

He was a preacher, had been off and on—mostly on—for 40 years or so. I suppose I must have heard him preach, but don't remember. But if the testimony of all who knew him is true, he did not run the usual Baptist gamut from hellfire to brimstone in the pulpit every Sunday, but walked a meeker path toward his maker, professing instead love and good sense and good humor and compassion in this dark world and wide. I was told he filled his pulpit with joy—even, I thought, if only the joy of a repetitive series of bad jokes; but even bad jokes may be a better road to heaven than the road of rusty nails and broken glass that many travel.

Two weeks before Christmas he died. At the funeral gathered family and friends and flock, and we who hadn't seen one another since 1968 mixed and mingled during the wake in Picayune, catching up with old times while Alton presided, supine and serene, at the end of the room in a bank of light and flowers.

Above us all floated a face at once familiar and strange: here, there, moving in and out of various configurations of folks like an old friend. I knew the face but could not put a name to it; I assumed it was one of the hundreds of faces you see at such occasions, of people you know and have forgotten, some who will remember you and make you at least momentarily embarrassed that you have forgotten.

I finally gave up on my memory and asked someone; he was Singing Billy Walker, whose face I knew not from among forgotten family and friends but from the several occasions of a channel-flicking Saturday night when I would light on the new Lawrence Welkized Grand Ole Opry on the Nashville Network or some such program of country and western and/or gospel singing. And then I remembered that during his off times from being a preacher, and recurrently during the on times too, Alton had wanted most of all to be a country music singer. He played guitar and sang with several different bands most of his life.

One of my most pleasant memories of Alton, of my childhood in fact, is of a moment in, say, 1953, when he was for a time a disc jockey on a country radio station in the Arkansas Ozarks. Very early one freezing Saturday morning he took me with him to the studio and I sat utterly enchanted while he played the hillbilly hits of the day, singing along at the top of his voice with Hank and Red and Ernest and Little Jimmy and other heroes of mine, in the intervals between records carrying on his irrepressible chatter with an invisible audience about music, about sales at the feed store, the weather, the crops, discounts at the five and dime that was to my ten-year-old ears completely magical and wonderfully connected to all things seen and unseen. I was rapt: it all sprang as an ecstasy out of his constant easy goofy spontaneous and extraordinary trademark grin, which was somehow contained in a voice that must have warmed many an Ozark kitchen, as it warmed me that freezing Ozark morning.

Alton had met Billy Walker during that time in Arkansas and they had remained very close friends for forty years. Walker was in Picayune because he was also a lay preacher; Alton had asked him to preach his funeral sermon.

The day of the funeral we gathered in the little church Alton had pastored up until the cancer had made it impossible. The church was overflowing, and Walker preached as Alton had asked him to, a celebration of his life, not a dirge for his passing: no brimstone or admonitions to salvation, which are de rigueur on such occasions. He sang two gospel tunes, also as Alton had requested; he brought along his guitar and a prerecorded musical background, and I wondered how many in the congregation had ever heard of karaoke. He talked a bit and sang, professional and cool and sure of his audience; talked a bit more and sang again, a rouser this time that he asked us to sing and clap along with. I couldn't bring myself actually to clap, but my knees bumped and my soft-soled shoes tapped silently on the floor and I, ever the observer, found myself drawn into the moment. I thought of how proudly and with what pleasure Alton had provided such a moment for us all.

Afterwards, after the burial, at the final gathering at dinner, across the road from the cemetery, I stood in Durscherl's kitchen and ate with family members, saying goodbye, probably until somebody else died and called us together. I kept an eye and an ear on Walker, who made his ministerial rounds, then got himself a plate of dumplings and sat at table chatting, visiting, talking about Alton in the old days, forty years ago, when he, Walker, was just getting started in the country music business. He talked lovingly of those old days and I thought I heard him speak of Hank Williams, of having sung with or known *Hank*. When someone vacated a place at the table, I drifted over and sat, to listen: not to confirm that I had heard right, because I didn't want to take the chance that I had heard wrong. I sat and listened and felt as one might have felt who chatted with Adam in his last years, not to talk *about* God in the old days but just to shake the hand of one who had shaken The Hand: touching base, getting connected.

That night I dreamed that Billy Walker introduced me to Hank backstage before a performance in the old Ryman Auditorium and, as people in dreams will, Hank asked me to sing with him. On stage I sang harmony to Hank's melody on *Precious Memories* and *Whispering Hope*, to a crowd hushed almost to tears. Alton sat in the front row, his great big hungry eyes popping with pleasure for me, his mouth stretched into that cheshire grin, as though there were only one place on earth he'd rather be. For encore Hank and I broke into a genuine handclapping singalong classic:

> This world is not my home, I'm just a-passing through.
> My treasures are laid up somewhere beyond the blue.
> The angels beckon me from heaven's open door,
> And I can't feel at home in this world any more.
>
> Oh Lord, You know, I have no friend like You.
> If heaven's not my home, then Lord what will I do?
> The angels beckon me from heaven's open door,
> And I can't feel at home in this world any more.

When we finished it was Alton who sang onstage with Hank and I who sat in the front row with my mother, legions of grandparents, aunts and uncles and cousins galore, grinning and clapping and singing along ecstatically at the top of my rejoicing soul, in the sweet grace of that great community.

It was a most satisfying funeral.